# Pillow Talk

*Awakened with Purpose*

## Intimate Conversations with God

*Atosha Logan*

# Pillow Talk

*Awakened with Purpose*

## Intimate Conversations with God

*Atosha Logan*

FOR PERMISSION REQUESTS, CONTACT THE AUTHOR AT:
ATOSHA LOGAN, AUTHOR & PUBLISHER
INFO@ATOSHALOGAN.COM
WWW.ATOSHALOGAN.COM

ISBN:979-8-9931753-4-8 (PAPERBACK)

PRINTED IN THE UNITED STATES OF AMERICA

COVER DESIGN: ATOSHA LOGAN
INTERIOR LAYOUT: ATOSHA LOGAN

ALL SCRIPTURES ARE TRANSLATED INTO THE NEW INTERNATIONAL VERSION VERSION (NIV) UNLESS OTHERWISE NOTED.

# *Pillow Talk*

## THIS JOURNAL BELONGS TO:

_____

_____

_____

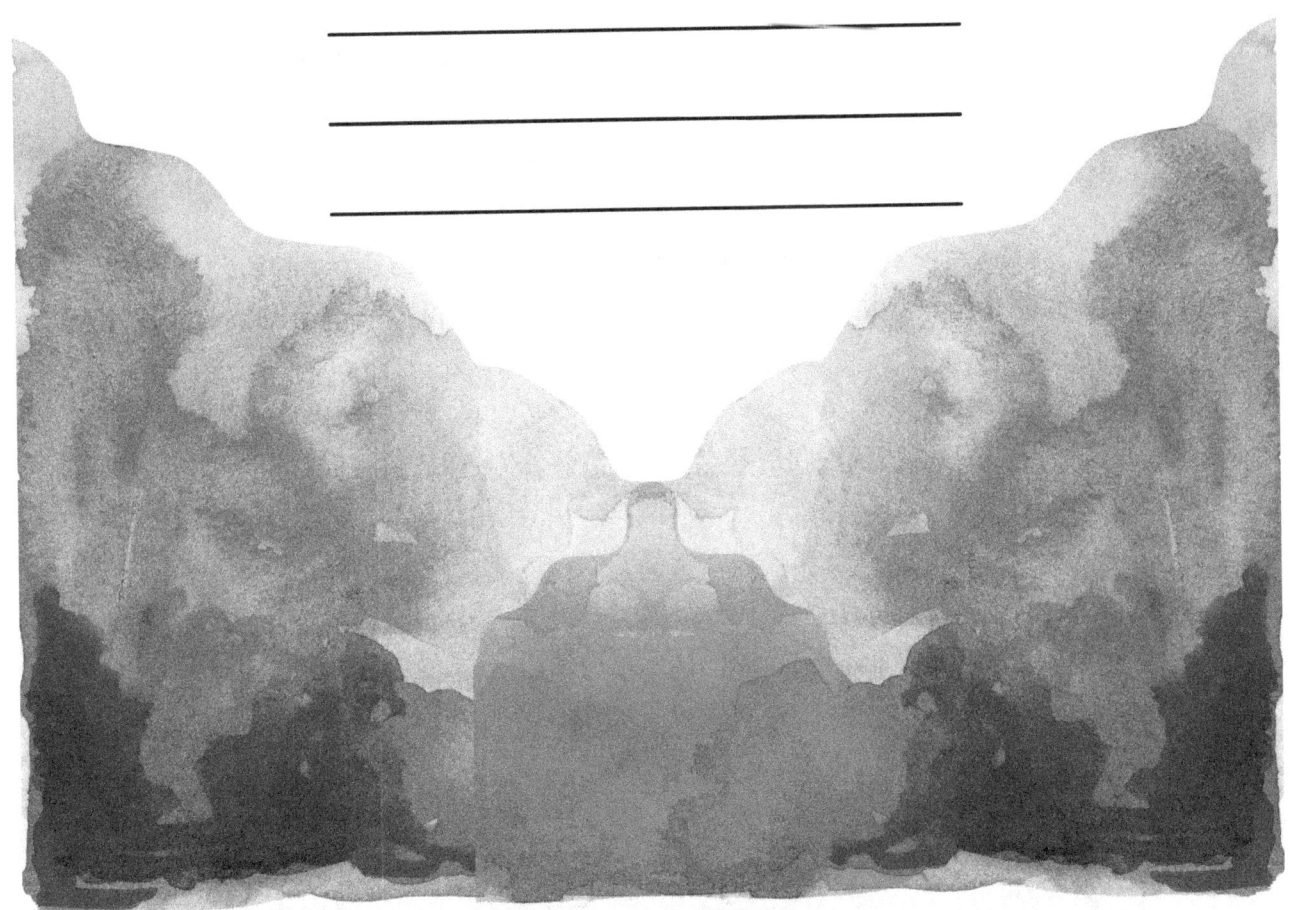

# Prophetic Insight

God uses dreams to communicate with His people.
Blending Scripture, testimony, and practical guidance, prophetic insight
helps readers discern divine messages in the stillness of the night and
respond with obedience and understanding.

Each prophetic insight leads you deeper into the sacred conversation
between God and His children:

*Sacred Slumber:* Understanding how and why God speaks through dreams.

*The Language of Heaven:* Interpreting the symbols and emotions that
appear in your sleep.

*When Dreams Warn and Direct:* Recognizing dreams of guidance,
protection, or spiritual warfare.

*Discerning God's Voice:* Separating divine revelation from personal
imagination.

*Write the Vision:* Recording, interpreting, and praying through what you
see.

*Awakened Purpose:* Turning revelation into real-life transformation.

The book is also designed as a reflective journal, giving space to record
dreams, connect them to Scripture, and listen more deeply for God's
direction.

Ultimately, **Pillow Talk** reminds you that rest is not silence; it is
conversation. Your dreams are not distractions; they are divine downloads
meant to shape your destiny, comfort your heart, and awaken your spirit.

*God's voice doesn't stop when you sleep;*
*He simply changes His tone.*

# Scriptural Reference

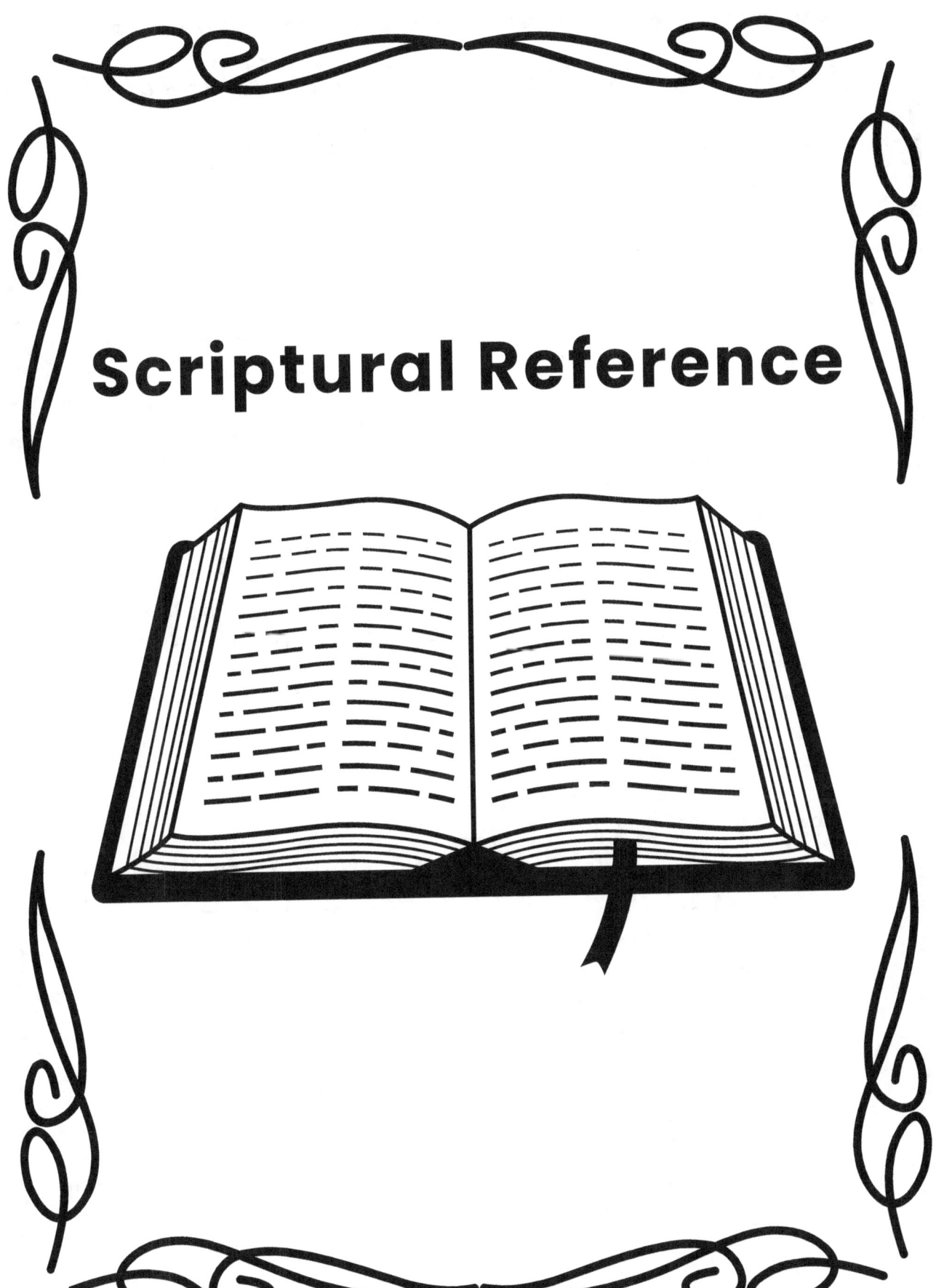

# Hearing God in Your Dreams

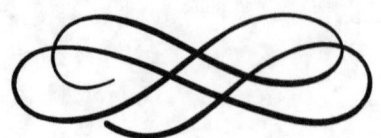

## Job 33:14–15 (NIV)

"For God does speak—now one way, now another—though no one perceives it. In a dream, in a vision of the night, when deep sleep falls on people as they slumber in their beds."

Reflection:
God still speaks through dreams — they are divine interruptions meant to awaken spiritual awareness.

## Genesis 28:12 (NIV)

"He had a dream in which he saw a stairway resting on the earth, with its top reaching to heaven, and the angels of God were ascending and descending on it."

Reflection:
Jacob's dream reminds us that God uses dreams to bridge heaven and earth — to remind us of His covenant and presence.

## John 10:27 (NIV)

"My sheep listen to my voice; I know them, and they follow me."

Reflection:
When God speaks, it's always personal. Those who walk closely with Him recognize His tone, whether awake or asleep.

## Daniel 2:19 (NIV)

"During the night the mystery was revealed to Daniel in a vision. Then Daniel praised the God of heaven."

Reflection:
Dreams are not confusion for the believer; they are mysteries revealed through prayer and praise.

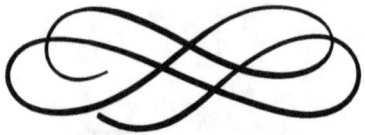

# Hearing God in Your Dreams

## Matthew 1:20 (NIV)

"But after he had considered this, an angel of the Lord appeared to him in a dream and said, 'Joseph son of David, do not be afraid to take Mary home as your wife.'"

Reflection:
God uses dreams to give direction, calm fears, and align our hearts with His plan.

## Daniel 4:5 (NIV)

"I had a dream that made me afraid. As I was lying in bed, the images and visions that passed through my mind terrified me."

Reflection:
Even troubling dreams can carry divine meaning — they call us to seek God's interpretation and wisdom.

## Matthew 2:19–20 (NIV)

"After Herod died, an angel of the Lord appeared in a dream to Joseph in Egypt and said, 'Get up, take the child and his mother and go to the land of Israel.'"

Reflection:
Dreams can carry life-saving instructions — obedience to divine direction always leads to protection.

## 1 Kings 3:5 (NIV)

"At Gibeon the Lord appeared to Solomon during the night in a dream, and God said, 'Ask for whatever you want me to give you.'"

Reflection:
God's invitations sometimes arrive at night — in dreams that open doors to purpose, wisdom, and divine favor.

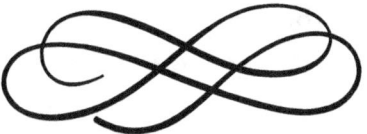

# Hearing God in Your Dreams

## Ecclesiastes 5:3, 7 (NIV)

"A dream comes when there are many cares... Much dreaming and many words are meaningless. Therefore, fear God."

Reflection:
Not every dream is divine — discernment is essential. Seek God, not merely the dream.

## Matthew 2:12 (NIV)

"And having been warned in a dream not to go back to Herod, they returned to their country by another route."

Reflection:
Sometimes dreams protect us — God redirects our path to keep us from unseen danger.

## Revelation 3:20 (NIV)

"Here I am! I stand at the door and knock. If anyone hears My voice and opens the door, I will come in and eat with that person, and they with Me."

Reflection:
God's voice invites intimacy. Every dream could be an invitation to deeper communion with Him.

## Daniel 7:1 (NIV)

"In the first year of Belshazzar king of Babylon, Daniel had a dream, and visions passed through his mind as he was lying in bed. He wrote down the substance of his dream."

Reflection:
The call to write down the dream in this journal is a revelation that deserves remembrance.

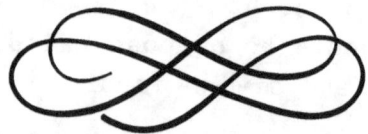

# Prophetic Numbers

| Number | Biblical Meaning | Spiritual Significance / Dream Reflection | Scripture Reference |
|--------|------------------|-------------------------------------------|---------------------|
| 1 | Unity & Beginning | God's sovereignty, new beginnings, wholeness, and divine authority. | *Ephesians 4:4–6; Genesis 1:1* |
| 2 | Witness & Partnership | Agreement, confirmation, and covenant (God confirming His word). | *Amos 3:3; Matthew 18:19–20* |
| 3 | Divine Perfection & Resurrection | The Trinity, wholeness, and new life after completion. | *Matthew 28:19; Luke 24:7* |
| 4 | Creation & Universality | The earth (four directions), completion of the natural world, stability. | *Revelation 7:1; Genesis 2:10* |
| 5 | Grace & Favor | Divine grace, redemption, and God's goodness toward humankind. | *Genesis 43:34; John 1:16* |
| 6 | Humanity & Labor | Man's weakness, imperfection, and human effort (created on day six). | *Revelation 13:18; Genesis 1:27* |
| 7 | Spiritual Perfection & Completion | God's finished work, divine rest, and covenant fulfillment. | *Genesis 2:2–3; Revelation 1:20* |
| 8 | New Beginnings & Resurrection | Renewal, restoration, and regeneration (new creation in Christ). | *Genesis 17:12; 2 Corinthians 5:17* |
| 9 | Divine Fruitfulness & Judgment | Finality, harvest, gifts of the Spirit, and spiritual maturity. | *Galatians 5:22–23; Matthew 27:45* |
| 10 | Order & Law | Responsibility, divine order, and government (Ten Commandments). | *Exodus 20:1–17; Matthew 25:1–13* |
| 11 | Disorder & Transition | Testing, chaos before completion, prophetic awakening. | *Genesis 37:9; Acts 1:26* |
| 12 | Authority & Divine Government | Spiritual structure, leadership, tribes, and apostolic power. | *Revelation 21:12–14; Luke 22:30* |

# Prophetic Symbols

| Symbol | Meaning | Spiritual Reflection | Scripture Reference |
|---|---|---|---|
| Water | Spirit, Cleansing, Renewal | God's presence or emotional cleansing. | *John 7:38; Ephesians 5:26* |
| Fire | Purification, Power, Judgment | Represents passion, testing, or the Holy Spirit. | *Acts 2:3; Exodus 3:2* |
| Light | Revelation, Truth, Direction | God's guidance or the unveiling of hidden things. | *Psalm 119:105; John 8:12* |
| Keys | Authority, Access, Revelation | Spiritual unlocking or new opportunities. | *Matthew 16:19; Revelation 3:7* |
| Doors / Gates | Transition, Opportunity, Boundaries | Indicates new beginnings or divine openings/closings. | *John 10:9; Revelation 3:8; Genesis 7:16* |
| Mountains | Challenges, Presence of God | Symbol of strength, prayer, or divine encounter. | *Isaiah 2:2–3; Matthew 17:1–2* |
| Wind | Spirit, Change, Movement | Represents the Holy Spirit or spiritual shifts. | *John 3:8; Acts 2:2* |
| Trees | Growth, Life, Generations | Symbolizes legacy, stability, and fruitfulness. | *Psalm 1:3; Jeremiah 17:8* |
| Snakes / Serpent | Deception, Temptation | Represents spiritual attack or hidden danger. | *Genesis 3:1–5; Luke 10:19* |
| Lions | Strength, Courage, Dominion | Can represent Christ (Lion of Judah) or threats | *Revelation 5:5; 1 Peter 5:8* |
| Oil | Anointing, Healing, Spirit | Divine favor, consecration, or empowerment. | *Psalm 23:5; James 5:14* |
| Rain | Blessing, Refreshing, Harvest | Renewal and the outpouring of the Spirit. | *Joel 2:23; Zechariah 10:1* |
| Bread | Word of God, Sustenance | Represents spiritual nourishment or revelation. | *John 6:35; Matthew 4:4* |
| Birds | Messages, Freedom, Spirit | Can symbolize divine messages or watchfulness. | *Matthew 6:26; Genesis 8:11* |
| Road / Path | Journey, Direction, Purpose | Represents life's choices and divine guidance. | *Proverbs 3:6; Isaiah 30:21* |
| Crown | Victory, Reward, Authority | Symbolizes achievement, calling, or eternal reward. | *2 Timothy 4:8; Revelation 2:10* |

# Prophetic Colors

| Color | Biblical Meaning | Spiritual Significance or Dream Reflection | Scripture Reference |
|---|---|---|---|
| White | Purity, Holiness, Victory | Represents righteousness, divine presence, and heavenly glory. | *Revelation 3:5; Isaiah 1:18* |
| Black | Mystery, Mourning, Sin | Can symbolize hidden things, death, or deep reflection. | *Lamentations 5:10; Job 30:30* |
| Red | Blood, Sacrifice, Passion | Represents Jesus' sacrifice, redemption, and divine love. | *Isaiah 1:18; Revelation 6:4* |
| Blue | Heaven, Revelation, Spirit | Often connected to heavenly insight, truth, and divine revelation. | *Exodus 24:10; Numbers 15:38–39* |
| Purple | Royalty, Majesty, Authority | The color of kingship, spiritual dominion, and wealth. | *John 19:2; Esther 8:15* |
| Gold | Glory, Divinity, Refinement | Symbolizes God's presence, eternal value, and purity through testing. | *Revelation 21:18; Malachi 3:3* |
| Green | Growth, Renewal, Prosperity | Signifies life, spiritual health, and new beginnings. | *Psalm 52:8; Revelation 9:4* |
| Yellow | Light, Glory, Faith | Represents divine illumination, joy, and wisdom. | *Exodus 25:31–40; Matthew 17:2* |
| Silver | Redemption, Refinement | Linked to purity, restoration, and divine testing. | *Psalm 66:10; Proverbs 25:11* |
| Brown | Humility, Earth, Foundation | Symbolizes humanity, endurance, and simplicity. | *Genesis 2:7; Isaiah 40:8* |
| Gray | Transition, Balance, Wisdom | Often represents aging, neutrality, or divine timing. | *Proverbs 16:31* |

# AWAKENED WITH PURPOSE

*Every dream is personal — seek God's Word and the Holy Spirit for confirmation.*

**Date:**                **Time:**                **Dream Title:**

**Dream Description**

**Scriptural Connection**

**Prayer of Revelation**
Lord, reveal what You are saying through this dream. Help me to walk in obedience and discern Your will clearly.

**Images/Symbols/Numbers**

**Interpretation/Discernment**

**Emotional Reflection:**

**Action Steps/Application:**
- ◯
- ◯
- ◯
- ◯
- ◯

**Confirmation Notes (Follow Up):**

# AWAKENED WITH PURPOSE

*Every dream is personal — seek God's Word and the Holy Spirit for confirmation.*

**Date:**          **Time:**                    **Dream Title:**

**Dream Description**

**Scriptural Connection**

**Prayer of Revelation**
Lord, reveal what You are saying through this dream. Help me to walk in obedience and discern Your will clearly.

**Images/Symbols/Numbers**

**Interpretation/Discernment**

**Emotional Reflection:**

**Action Steps/Application:**
- ◯
- ◯
- ◯
- ◯
- ◯

**Confirmation Notes (Follow Up):**

# AWAKENED WITH PURPOSE

*Every dream is personal — seek God's Word and the Holy Spirit for confirmation.*

**Date:**                    **Time:**                    **Dream Title:**

**Dream Description**

**Scriptural Connection**

**Prayer of Revelation**
Lord, reveal what You are saying through this dream. Help me to walk in obedience and discern Your will clearly.

**Images/Symbols/Numbers**

**Interpretation/Discernment**

**Emotional Reflection:**

**Action Steps/Application:**
- ○
- ○
- ○
- ○
- ○

**Confirmation Notes (Follow Up):**

# AWAKENED WITH PURPOSE

*Every dream is personal — seek God's Word and the Holy Spirit for confirmation.*

**Date:**                    **Time:**                    **Dream Title:**

**Dream Description**

**Scriptural Connection**

**Prayer of Revelation**

Lord, reveal what You are saying through this dream. Help me to walk in obedience and discern Your will clearly.

**Images/Symbols/Numbers**

**Interpretation/Discernment**

**Emotional Reflection:**

**Action Steps/Application:**

○
○
○
○
○

**Confirmation Notes (Follow Up):**

# AWAKENED WITH PURPOSE

*Every dream is personal — seek God's Word and the Holy Spirit for confirmation.*

**Date:**      **Time:**      **Dream Title:**

**Dream Description**

**Scriptural Connection**

**Prayer of Revelation**
Lord, reveal what You are saying through this dream. Help me to walk in obedience and discern Your will clearly.

**Images/Symbols/Numbers**

**Interpretation/Discernment**

**Emotional Reflection:**

**Action Steps/Application:**
- ⭘
- ⭘
- ⭘
- ⭘
- ⭘

**Confirmation Notes (Follow Up):**

# AWAKENED WITH PURPOSE

*Every dream is personal — seek God's Word and the Holy Spirit for confirmation.*

**Date:**      **Time:**      **Dream Title:**

**Dream Description**

**Scriptural Connection**

**Prayer of Revelation**

Lord, reveal what You are saying through this dream. Help me to walk in obedience and discern Your will clearly.

**Images/Symbols/Numbers**

**Interpretation/Discernment**

**Emotional Reflection:**

**Action Steps/Application:**

○
○
○
○
○

**Confirmation Notes (Follow Up):**

# AWAKENED WITH PURPOSE

*Every dream is personal — seek God's Word and the Holy Spirit for confirmation.*

**Date:**　　　　　**Time:**　　　　　**Dream Title:**

**Dream Description**

**Scriptural Connection**

**Prayer of Revelation**

Lord, reveal what You are saying through this dream. Help me to walk in obedience and discern Your will clearly.

**Images/Symbols/Numbers**

**Interpretation/Discernment**

**Emotional Reflection:**

**Action Steps/Application:**

○
○
○
○
○

**Confirmation Notes (Follow Up):**

# AWAKENED WITH PURPOSE

*Every dream is personal — seek God's Word and the Holy Spirit for confirmation.*

**Date:**   **Time:**   **Dream Title:**

**Dream Description**

**Scriptural Connection**

**Prayer of Revelation**

Lord, reveal what You are saying through this dream. Help me to walk in obedience and discern Your will clearly.

**Images/Symbols/Numbers**

**Interpretation/Discernment**

**Emotional Reflection:**

**Action Steps/Application:**

○
○
○
○
○

**Confirmation Notes (Follow Up):**

# AWAKENED WITH PURPOSE

*Every dream is personal — seek God's Word and the Holy Spirit for confirmation.*

**Date:**                **Time:**                **Dream Title:**

**Dream Description**

**Scriptural Connection**

**Prayer of Revelation**
Lord, reveal what You are saying through this dream. Help me to walk in obedience and discern Your will clearly.

**Images/Symbols/Numbers**

**Interpretation/Discernment**

**Emotional Reflection:**

**Action Steps/Application:**
- ○
- ○
- ○
- ○
- ○

**Confirmation Notes (Follow Up):**

# AWAKENED WITH PURPOSE

*Every dream is personal — seek God's Word and the Holy Spirit for confirmation.*

Date:                    Time:                    Dream Title:

**Dream Description**

**Scriptural Connection**

**Prayer of Revelation**

Lord, reveal what You are saying through this dream. Help me to walk in obedience and discern Your will clearly.

**Images/Symbols/Numbers**

**Interpretation/Discernment**

**Emotional Reflection:**

**Action Steps/Application:**
- ○
- ○
- ○
- ○
- ○

**Confirmation Notes (Follow Up):**

# AWAKENED WITH PURPOSE

*Every dream is personal — seek God's Word and the Holy Spirit for confirmation.*

**Date:**      **Time:**      **Dream Title:**

**Dream Description**

**Scriptural Connection**

## Prayer of Revelation

Lord, reveal what You are saying through this dream. Help me to walk in obedience and discern Your will clearly.

**Images/Symbols/Numbers**

**Interpretation/Discernment**

**Emotional Reflection:**

**Action Steps/Application:**
- ◯
- ◯
- ◯
- ◯
- ◯

**Confirmation Notes (Follow Up):**

# AWAKENED WITH PURPOSE

*Every dream is personal — seek God's Word and the Holy Spirit for confirmation.*

**Date:**                **Time:**                **Dream Title:**

**Dream Description**

**Scriptural Connection**

### Prayer of Revelation

Lord, reveal what You are saying through this dream. Help me to walk in obedience and discern Your will clearly.

**Images/Symbols/Numbers**

**Interpretation/Discernment**

**Emotional Reflection:**

**Action Steps/Application:**
- ○
- ○
- ○
- ○
- ○

**Confirmation Notes (Follow Up):**

# AWAKENED WITH PURPOSE

*Every dream is personal — seek God's Word and the Holy Spirit for confirmation.*

**Date:**        **Time:**        **Dream Title:**

**Dream Description**

**Scriptural Connection**

**Prayer of Revelation**
Lord, reveal what You are saying through this dream. Help me to walk in obedience and discern Your will clearly.

**Images/Symbols/Numbers**

**Interpretation/Discernment**

**Emotional Reflection:**

**Action Steps/Application:**
- ○
- ○
- ○
- ○
- ○

**Confirmation Notes (Follow Up):**

# AWAKENED WITH PURPOSE

*Every dream is personal — seek God's Word and the Holy Spirit for confirmation.*

**Date:**                    **Time:**                    **Dream Title:**

**Dream Description**

**Scriptural Connection**

**Prayer of Revelation**

Lord, reveal what You are saying through this dream. Help me to walk in obedience and discern Your will clearly.

**Images/Symbols/Numbers**

**Interpretation/Discernment**

**Emotional Reflection:**

**Action Steps/Application:**

○
○
○
○
○

**Confirmation Notes (Follow Up):**

# AWAKENED WITH PURPOSE

*Every dream is personal — seek God's Word and the Holy Spirit for confirmation.*

**Date:**                    **Time:**                    **Dream Title:**

**Dream Description**                                                    **Scriptural Connection**

**Prayer of Revelation**

Lord, reveal what You are saying through this dream. Help me to walk in obedience and discern Your will clearly.

**Images/Symbols/Numbers**                                              **Interpretation/Discernment**

**Emotional Reflection:**

**Action Steps/Application:**                          **Confirmation Notes (Follow Up):**

○
○
○
○
○

# AWAKENED WITH PURPOSE

*Every dream is personal — seek God's Word and the Holy Spirit for confirmation.*

**Date:**  **Time:**  **Dream Title:**

**Dream Description**

**Scriptural Connection**

**Prayer of Revelation**

Lord, reveal what You are saying through this dream. Help me to walk in obedience and discern Your will clearly.

**Images/Symbols/Numbers**

**Interpretation/Discernment**

**Emotional Reflection:**

**Action Steps/Application:**

- ◯
- ◯
- ◯
- ◯
- ◯

**Confirmation Notes (Follow Up):**

# AWAKENED WITH PURPOSE

*Every dream is personal — seek God's Word and the Holy Spirit for confirmation.*

**Date:**      **Time:**      **Dream Title:**

**Dream Description**

**Scriptural Connection**

**Prayer of Revelation**
Lord, reveal what You are saying through this dream. Help me to walk in obedience and discern Your will clearly.

**Images/Symbols/Numbers**

**Interpretation/Discernment**

**Emotional Reflection:**

**Action Steps/Application:**
- ○
- ○
- ○
- ○
- ○

**Confirmation Notes (Follow Up):**

# AWAKENED WITH PURPOSE

*Every dream is personal — seek God's Word and the Holy Spirit for confirmation.*

**Date:**                **Time:**                **Dream Title:**

**Dream Description**

**Scriptural Connection**

**Prayer of Revelation**

Lord, reveal what You are saying through this dream. Help me to walk in obedience and discern Your will clearly.

**Images/Symbols/Numbers**

**Interpretation/Discernment**

**Emotional Reflection:**

**Action Steps/Application:**

- ○
- ○
- ○
- ○
- ○

**Confirmation Notes (Follow Up):**

# AWAKENED WITH PURPOSE

*Every dream is personal — seek God's Word and the Holy Spirit for confirmation.*

**Date:**  **Time:**  **Dream Title:**

**Dream Description**

**Scriptural Connection**

**Prayer of Revelation**

Lord, reveal what You are saying through this dream. Help me to walk in obedience and discern Your will clearly.

**Images/Symbols/Numbers**

**Interpretation/Discernment**

**Emotional Reflection:**

**Action Steps/Application:**
- ○
- ○
- ○
- ○
- ○

**Confirmation Notes (Follow Up):**

# AWAKENED WITH PURPOSE

*Every dream is personal — seek God's Word and the Holy Spirit for confirmation.*

**Date:**                    **Time:**                    **Dream Title:**

**Dream Description**

**Scriptural Connection**

**Prayer of Revelation**

Lord, reveal what You are saying through this dream. Help me to walk in obedience and discern Your will clearly.

**Images/Symbols/Numbers**

**Interpretation/Discernment**

**Emotional Reflection:**

**Action Steps/Application:**

○
○
○
○
○

**Confirmation Notes (Follow Up):**

# AWAKENED WITH PURPOSE

*Every dream is personal — seek God's Word and the Holy Spirit for confirmation.*

**Date:**     **Time:**     **Dream Title:**

**Dream Description**

**Scriptural Connection**

**Prayer of Revelation**
Lord, reveal what You are saying through this dream. Help me to walk in obedience and discern Your will clearly.

**Images/Symbols/Numbers**

**Interpretation/Discernment**

**Emotional Reflection:**

**Action Steps/Application:**
- ○
- ○
- ○
- ○
- ○

**Confirmation Notes (Follow Up):**

# AWAKENED WITH PURPOSE

*Every dream is personal — seek God's Word and the Holy Spirit for confirmation.*

Date:                Time:                Dream Title:

**Dream Description**

**Scriptural Connection**

**Prayer of Revelation**

Lord, reveal what You are saying through this dream. Help me to walk in obedience and discern Your will clearly.

**Images/Symbols/Numbers**

**Interpretation/Discernment**

**Emotional Reflection:**

**Action Steps/Application:**
- ○
- ○
- ○
- ○
- ○

**Confirmation Notes (Follow Up):**

# AWAKENED WITH PURPOSE

*Every dream is personal — seek God's Word and the Holy Spirit for confirmation.*

**Date:**     **Time:**     **Dream Title:**

**Dream Description**

**Scriptural Connection**

**Prayer of Revelation**
Lord, reveal what You are saying through this dream. Help me to walk in obedience and discern Your will clearly.

**Images/Symbols/Numbers**

**Interpretation/Discernment**

**Emotional Reflection:**

**Action Steps/Application:**
○
○
○
○
○

**Confirmation Notes (Follow Up):**

# AWAKENED WITH PURPOSE

*Every dream is personal — seek God's Word and the Holy Spirit for confirmation.*

**Date:**                **Time:**                **Dream Title:**

**Dream Description**

**Scriptural Connection**

### Prayer of Revelation
Lord, reveal what You are saying through this dream. Help me to walk in obedience and discern Your will clearly.

**Images/Symbols/Numbers**

**Interpretation/Discernment**

**Emotional Reflection:**

**Action Steps/Application:**
- ○
- ○
- ○
- ○
- ○

**Confirmation Notes (Follow Up):**

# AWAKENED WITH PURPOSE

*Every dream is personal — seek God's Word and the Holy Spirit for confirmation.*

Date:                Time:                Dream Title:

**Dream Description**

**Scriptural Connection**

**Prayer of Revelation**
Lord, reveal what You are saying through this dream. Help me to walk in obedience and discern Your will clearly.

**Images/Symbols/Numbers**

**Interpretation/Discernment**

**Emotional Reflection:**

**Action Steps/Application:**
- ○
- ○
- ○
- ○
- ○

**Confirmation Notes (Follow Up):**

# AWAKENED WITH PURPOSE

*Every dream is personal — seek God's Word and the Holy Spirit for confirmation.*

**Date:**                **Time:**                **Dream Title:**

**Dream Description**

**Scriptural Connection**

**Prayer of Revelation**

Lord, reveal what You are saying through this dream. Help me to walk in obedience and discern Your will clearly.

**Images/Symbols/Numbers**

**Interpretation/Discernment**

**Emotional Reflection:**

**Action Steps/Application:**

○
○
○
○
○

**Confirmation Notes (Follow Up):**

# AWAKENED WITH PURPOSE

*Every dream is personal — seek God's Word and the Holy Spirit for confirmation.*

**Date:**      **Time:**      **Dream Title:**

**Dream Description**

**Scriptural Connection**

**Prayer of Revelation**

Lord, reveal what You are saying through this dream. Help me to walk in obedience and discern Your will clearly.

**Images/Symbols/Numbers**

**Interpretation/Discernment**

**Emotional Reflection:**

**Action Steps/Application:**
- ◯
- ◯
- ◯
- ◯
- ◯

**Confirmation Notes (Follow Up):**

# AWAKENED WITH PURPOSE

*Every dream is personal — seek God's Word and the Holy Spirit for confirmation.*

**Date:**      **Time:**      **Dream Title:**

**Dream Description**

**Scriptural Connection**

**Prayer of Revelation**

Lord, reveal what You are saying through this dream. Help me to walk in obedience and discern Your will clearly.

**Images/Symbols/Numbers**

**Interpretation/Discernment**

**Emotional Reflection:**

**Action Steps/Application:**
- ○
- ○
- ○
- ○
- ○

**Confirmation Notes (Follow Up):**

# AWAKENED WITH PURPOSE

*Every dream is personal — seek God's Word and the Holy Spirit for confirmation.*

**Date:**                **Time:**                **Dream Title:**

**Dream Description**

**Scriptural Connection**

**Prayer of Revelation**
Lord, reveal what You are saying through this dream. Help me to walk in obedience and discern Your will clearly.

**Images/Symbols/Numbers**

**Interpretation/Discernment**

**Emotional Reflection:**

**Action Steps/Application:**
- ○
- ○
- ○
- ○
- ○

**Confirmation Notes (Follow Up):**

# AWAKENED WITH PURPOSE

*Every dream is personal — seek God's Word and the Holy Spirit for confirmation.*

Date:                    Time:                    Dream Title:

**Dream Description**

**Scriptural Connection**

**Prayer of Revelation**

Lord, reveal what You are saying through this dream. Help me to walk in obedience and discern Your will clearly.

**Images/Symbols/Numbers**

**Interpretation/Discernment**

**Emotional Reflection:**

**Action Steps/Application:**

○
○
○
○
○

**Confirmation Notes (Follow Up):**

# AWAKENED WITH PURPOSE

*Every dream is personal — seek God's Word and the Holy Spirit for confirmation.*

**Date:** **Time:** **Dream Title:**

**Dream Description**

**Scriptural Connection**

**Prayer of Revelation**

Lord, reveal what You are saying through this dream. Help me to walk in obedience and discern Your will clearly.

**Images/Symbols/Numbers**

**Interpretation/Discernment**

**Emotional Reflection:**

**Action Steps/Application:**

- ○
- ○
- ○
- ○
- ○

**Confirmation Notes (Follow Up):**

# AWAKENED WITH PURPOSE

*Every dream is personal — seek God's Word and the Holy Spirit for confirmation.*

**Date:**       **Time:**       **Dream Title:**

**Dream Description**

**Scriptural Connection**

### Prayer of Revelation
Lord, reveal what You are saying through this dream. Help me to walk in obedience and discern Your will clearly.

**Images/Symbols/Numbers**

**Interpretation/Discernment**

**Emotional Reflection:**

**Action Steps/Application:**
- ○
- ○
- ○
- ○
- ○

**Confirmation Notes (Follow Up):**

# AWAKENED WITH PURPOSE

*Every dream is personal — seek God's Word and the Holy Spirit for confirmation.*

**Date:**                **Time:**                **Dream Title:**

**Dream Description**

**Scriptural Connection**

### Prayer of Revelation
Lord, reveal what You are saying through this dream. Help me to walk in obedience and discern Your will clearly.

**Images/Symbols/Numbers**

**Interpretation/Discernment**

**Emotional Reflection:**

**Action Steps/Application:**
- ◯
- ◯
- ◯
- ◯
- ◯

**Confirmation Notes (Follow Up):**

# AWAKENED WITH PURPOSE

*Every dream is personal — seek God's Word and the Holy Spirit for confirmation.*

Date:                  Time:                  Dream Title:

**Dream Description**

**Scriptural Connection**

**Prayer of Revelation**

Lord, reveal what You are saying through this dream. Help me to walk in obedience and discern Your will clearly.

**Images/Symbols/Numbers**

**Interpretation/Discernment**

**Emotional Reflection:**

**Action Steps/Application:**

○
○
○
○
○

**Confirmation Notes (Follow Up):**

# AWAKENED WITH PURPOSE

*Every dream is personal — seek God's Word and the Holy Spirit for confirmation.*

Date:                    Time:                    Dream Title:

**Dream Description**

**Scriptural Connection**

**Prayer of Revelation**

Lord, reveal what You are saying through this dream. Help me to walk in obedience and discern Your will clearly.

**Images/Symbols/Numbers**

**Interpretation/Discernment**

**Emotional Reflection:**

**Action Steps/Application:**
- ◯
- ◯
- ◯
- ◯
- ◯

**Confirmation Notes (Follow Up):**

# AWAKENED WITH PURPOSE

*Every dream is personal — seek God's Word and the Holy Spirit for confirmation.*

**Date:**                **Time:**                **Dream Title:**

**Dream Description**

**Scriptural Connection**

**Prayer of Revelation**

Lord, reveal what You are saying through this dream. Help me to walk in obedience and discern Your will clearly.

**Images/Symbols/Numbers**

**Interpretation/Discernment**

**Emotional Reflection:**

**Action Steps/Application:**

- ○
- ○
- ○
- ○
- ○

**Confirmation Notes (Follow Up):**

# AWAKENED WITH PURPOSE

*Every dream is personal — seek God's Word and the Holy Spirit for confirmation.*

**Date:**      **Time:**      **Dream Title:**

**Dream Description**

**Scriptural Connection**

**Prayer of Revelation**
Lord, reveal what You are saying through this dream. Help me to walk in obedience and discern Your will clearly.

**Images/Symbols/Numbers**

**Interpretation/Discernment**

**Emotional Reflection:**

**Action Steps/Application:**
- ◯
- ◯
- ◯
- ◯
- ◯

**Confirmation Notes (Follow Up):**

# AWAKENED WITH PURPOSE

*Every dream is personal — seek God's Word and the Holy Spirit for confirmation.*

Date:                    Time:                    Dream Title:

**Dream Description**

**Scriptural Connection**

**Prayer of Revelation**

Lord, reveal what You are saying through this dream. Help me to walk in obedience and discern Your will clearly.

**Images/Symbols/Numbers**

**Interpretation/Discernment**

**Emotional Reflection:**

**Action Steps/Application:**

○
○
○
○
○

**Confirmation Notes (Follow Up):**

# AWAKENED WITH PURPOSE

*Every dream is personal — seek God's Word and the Holy Spirit for confirmation.*

**Date:** **Time:** **Dream Title:**

**Dream Description**

**Scriptural Connection**

**Prayer of Revelation**
Lord, reveal what You are saying through this dream. Help me to walk in obedience and discern Your will clearly.

**Images/Symbols/Numbers**

**Interpretation/Discernment**

**Emotional Reflection:**

**Action Steps/Application:**
- ○
- ○
- ○
- ○
- ○

**Confirmation Notes (Follow Up):**

# AWAKENED WITH PURPOSE

*Every dream is personal — seek God's Word and the Holy Spirit for confirmation.*

**Date:**      **Time:**      **Dream Title:**

**Dream Description**

**Scriptural Connection**

### Prayer of Revelation

Lord, reveal what You are saying through this dream. Help me to walk in obedience and discern Your will clearly.

**Images/Symbols/Numbers**

**Interpretation/Discernment**

**Emotional Reflection:**

**Action Steps/Application:**

- ◯
- ◯
- ◯
- ◯
- ◯

**Confirmation Notes (Follow Up):**

# AWAKENED WITH PURPOSE

*Every dream is personal — seek God's Word and the Holy Spirit for confirmation.*

**Date:**                **Time:**                **Dream Title:**

**Dream Description**

**Scriptural Connection**

**Prayer of Revelation**
Lord, reveal what You are saying through this dream. Help me to walk in obedience and discern Your will clearly.

**Images/Symbols/Numbers**

**Interpretation/Discernment**

**Emotional Reflection:**

**Action Steps/Application:**
- ○
- ○
- ○
- ○
- ○

**Confirmation Notes (Follow Up):**

# AWAKENED WITH PURPOSE

*Every dream is personal — seek God's Word and the Holy Spirit for confirmation.*

**Date:**                **Time:**                **Dream Title:**

**Dream Description**

**Scriptural Connection**

**Prayer of Revelation**

Lord, reveal what You are saying through this dream. Help me to walk in obedience and discern Your will clearly.

**Images/Symbols/Numbers**

**Interpretation/Discernment**

**Emotional Reflection:**

**Action Steps/Application:**

○
○
○
○
○

**Confirmation Notes (Follow Up):**

# AWAKENED WITH PURPOSE

*Every dream is personal — seek God's Word and the Holy Spirit for confirmation.*

**Date:**            **Time:**            **Dream Title:**

**Dream Description**

**Scriptural Connection**

### Prayer of Revelation
Lord, reveal what You are saying through this dream. Help me to walk in obedience and discern Your will clearly.

**Images/Symbols/Numbers**

**Interpretation/Discernment**

**Emotional Reflection:**

**Action Steps/Application:**
○
○
○
○
○

**Confirmation Notes (Follow Up):**

# AWAKENED WITH PURPOSE

*Every dream is personal — seek God's Word and the Holy Spirit for confirmation.*

Date:                Time:                Dream Title:

**Dream Description**

**Scriptural Connection**

**Prayer of Revelation**

Lord, reveal what You are saying through this dream. Help me to walk in obedience and discern Your will clearly.

**Images/Symbols/Numbers**

**Interpretation/Discernment**

**Emotional Reflection:**

**Action Steps/Application:**

○
○
○
○
○

**Confirmation Notes (Follow Up):**

# AWAKENED WITH PURPOSE

*Every dream is personal — seek God's Word and the Holy Spirit for confirmation.*

**Date:**        **Time:**        **Dream Title:**

**Dream Description**

**Scriptural Connection**

### Prayer of Revelation

Lord, reveal what You are saying through this dream. Help me to walk in obedience and discern Your will clearly.

**Images/Symbols/Numbers**

**Interpretation/Discernment**

**Emotional Reflection:**

**Action Steps/Application:**
- ◯
- ◯
- ◯
- ◯
- ◯

**Confirmation Notes (Follow Up):**

# AWAKENED WITH PURPOSE

*Every dream is personal — seek God's Word and the Holy Spirit for confirmation.*

**Date:**      **Time:**      **Dream Title:**

**Dream Description**

**Scriptural Connection**

### Prayer of Revelation

Lord, reveal what You are saying through this dream. Help me to walk in obedience and discern Your will clearly.

**Images/Symbols/Numbers**

**Interpretation/Discernment**

**Emotional Reflection:**

**Action Steps/Application:**

- ◯
- ◯
- ◯
- ◯
- ◯

**Confirmation Notes (Follow Up):**

# AWAKENED WITH PURPOSE

*Every dream is personal — seek God's Word and the Holy Spirit for confirmation.*

Date:      Time:      Dream Title:

**Dream Description**

**Scriptural Connection**

### Prayer of Revelation

Lord, reveal what You are saying through this dream. Help me to walk in obedience and discern Your will clearly.

**Images/Symbols/Numbers**

**Interpretation/Discernment**

**Emotional Reflection:**

**Action Steps/Application:**

○
○
○
○
○

**Confirmation Notes (Follow Up):**

# AWAKENED WITH PURPOSE

*Every dream is personal — seek God's Word and the Holy Spirit for confirmation.*

**Date:** **Time:** **Dream Title:**

**Dream Description**

**Scriptural Connection**

**Prayer of Revelation**
Lord, reveal what You are saying through this dream. Help me to walk in obedience and discern Your will clearly.

**Images/Symbols/Numbers**

**Interpretation/Discernment**

**Emotional Reflection:**

**Action Steps/Application:**

○
○
○
○
○

**Confirmation Notes (Follow Up):**

# AWAKENED WITH PURPOSE

*Every dream is personal — seek God's Word and the Holy Spirit for confirmation.*

**Date:**　　　　　**Time:**　　　　　**Dream Title:**

**Dream Description**

**Scriptural Connection**

### Prayer of Revelation
Lord, reveal what You are saying through this dream. Help me to walk in obedience and discern Your will clearly.

**Images/Symbols/Numbers**

**Interpretation/Discernment**

**Emotional Reflection:**

**Action Steps/Application:**
- ◯
- ◯
- ◯
- ◯
- ◯

**Confirmation Notes (Follow Up):**

# AWAKENED WITH PURPOSE

*Every dream is personal — seek God's Word and the Holy Spirit for confirmation.*

**Date:**        **Time:**        **Dream Title:**

**Dream Description**

**Scriptural Connection**

**Prayer of Revelation**

Lord, reveal what You are saying through this dream. Help me to walk in obedience and discern Your will clearly.

**Images/Symbols/Numbers**

**Interpretation/Discernment**

**Emotional Reflection:**

**Action Steps/Application:**

- ◯
- ◯
- ◯
- ◯
- ◯

**Confirmation Notes (Follow Up):**

# AWAKENED WITH PURPOSE

*Every dream is personal — seek God's Word and the Holy Spirit for confirmation.*

**Date:**      **Time:**      **Dream Title:**

**Dream Description**

**Scriptural Connection**

### Prayer of Revelation
Lord, reveal what You are saying through this dream. Help me to walk in obedience and discern Your will clearly.

**Images/Symbols/Numbers**

**Interpretation/Discernment**

**Emotional Reflection:**

**Action Steps/Application:**
- ◯
- ◯
- ◯
- ◯
- ◯

**Confirmation Notes (Follow Up):**

# AWAKENED WITH PURPOSE

*Every dream is personal — seek God's Word and the Holy Spirit for confirmation.*

Date:        Time:        Dream Title:

**Dream Description**

**Scriptural Connection**

### Prayer of Revelation
Lord, reveal what You are saying through this dream. Help me to walk in obedience and discern Your will clearly.

**Images/Symbols/Numbers**

**Interpretation/Discernment**

**Emotional Reflection:**

**Action Steps/Application:**
- ○
- ○
- ○
- ○
- ○

**Confirmation Notes (Follow Up):**

# AWAKENED WITH PURPOSE

*Every dream is personal — seek God's Word and the Holy Spirit for confirmation.*

**Date:**       **Time:**       **Dream Title:**

**Dream Description**

**Scriptural Connection**

**Prayer of Revelation**

Lord, reveal what You are saying through this dream. Help me to walk in obedience and discern Your will clearly.

**Images/Symbols/Numbers**

**Interpretation/Discernment**

**Emotional Reflection:**

**Action Steps/Application:**
- ○
- ○
- ○
- ○
- ○

**Confirmation Notes (Follow Up):**

# AWAKENED WITH PURPOSE

*Every dream is personal — seek God's Word and the Holy Spirit for confirmation.*

**Date:**                    **Time:**                         **Dream Title:**

**Dream Description**                                    **Scriptural Connection**

**Prayer of Revelation**

Lord, reveal what You are saying through this dream. Help me to walk in obedience and discern Your will clearly.

**Images/Symbols/Numbers**                    **Interpretation/Discernment**

**Emotional Reflection:**

**Action Steps/Application:**                         **Confirmation Notes (Follow Up):**

○
○
○
○
○

# AWAKENED WITH PURPOSE

*Every dream is personal — seek God's Word and the Holy Spirit for confirmation.*

**Date:**                    **Time:**                    **Dream Title:**

**Dream Description**

**Scriptural Connection**

**Prayer of Revelation**
Lord, reveal what You are saying through this dream. Help me to walk in obedience and discern Your will clearly.

**Images/Symbols/Numbers**

**Interpretation/Discernment**

**Emotional Reflection:**

**Action Steps/Application:**
- ○
- ○
- ○
- ○
- ○

**Confirmation Notes (Follow Up):**

# AWAKENED WITH PURPOSE

*Every dream is personal — seek God's Word and the Holy Spirit for confirmation.*

**Date:**          **Time:**          **Dream Title:**

**Dream Description**

**Scriptural Connection**

**Prayer of Revelation**

Lord, reveal what You are saying through this dream. Help me to walk in obedience and discern Your will clearly.

**Images/Symbols/Numbers**

**Interpretation/Discernment**

**Emotional Reflection:**

**Action Steps/Application:**

○
○
○
○
○

**Confirmation Notes (Follow Up):**

# AWAKENED WITH PURPOSE

*Every dream is personal — seek God's Word and the Holy Spirit for confirmation.*

**Date:**          **Time:**          **Dream Title:**

**Dream Description**

**Scriptural Connection**

**Prayer of Revelation**
Lord, reveal what You are saying through this dream. Help me to walk in obedience and discern Your will clearly.

**Images/Symbols/Numbers**

**Interpretation/Discernment**

**Emotional Reflection:**

**Action Steps/Application:**
- ○
- ○
- ○
- ○
- ○

**Confirmation Notes (Follow Up):**

# AWAKENED WITH PURPOSE

*Every dream is personal — seek God's Word and the Holy Spirit for confirmation.*

Date:                    Time:                    Dream Title:

**Dream Description**

**Scriptural Connection**

**Prayer of Revelation**
Lord, reveal what You are saying through this dream. Help me to walk in obedience and discern Your will clearly.

**Images/Symbols/Numbers**

**Interpretation/Discernment**

**Emotional Reflection:**

**Action Steps/Application:**
- ◯
- ◯
- ◯
- ◯
- ◯

**Confirmation Notes (Follow Up):**

# AWAKENED WITH PURPOSE

*Every dream is personal — seek God's Word and the Holy Spirit for confirmation.*

Date:      Time:      Dream Title:

**Dream Description**

**Scriptural Connection**

**Prayer of Revelation**
Lord, reveal what You are saying through this dream. Help me to walk in obedience and discern Your will clearly.

**Images/Symbols/Numbers**

**Interpretation/Discernment**

**Emotional Reflection:**

**Action Steps/Application:**
- ○
- ○
- ○
- ○
- ○

**Confirmation Notes (Follow Up):**

# AWAKENED WITH PURPOSE

*Every dream is personal — seek God's Word and the Holy Spirit for confirmation.*

**Date:**          **Time:**               **Dream Title:**

**Dream Description**

**Scriptural Connection**

**Prayer of Revelation**

Lord, reveal what You are saying through this dream. Help me to walk in obedience and discern Your will clearly.

**Images/Symbols/Numbers**

**Interpretation/Discernment**

**Emotional Reflection:**

**Action Steps/Application:**

○
○
○
○
○

**Confirmation Notes (Follow Up):**

# AWAKENED WITH PURPOSE

*Every dream is personal — seek God's Word and the Holy Spirit for confirmation.*

**Date:**         **Time:**         **Dream Title:**

**Dream Description**

**Scriptural Connection**

### Prayer of Revelation
Lord, reveal what You are saying through this dream. Help me to walk in obedience and discern Your will clearly.

**Images/Symbols/Numbers**

**Interpretation/Discernment**

**Emotional Reflection:**

**Action Steps/Application:**
- ○
- ○
- ○
- ○
- ○

**Confirmation Notes (Follow Up):**

# AWAKENED WITH PURPOSE

*Every dream is personal — seek God's Word and the Holy Spirit for confirmation.*

**Date:**                **Time:**                **Dream Title:**

**Dream Description**                                    **Scriptural Connection**

**Prayer of Revelation**

Lord, reveal what You are saying through this dream. Help me to walk in obedience and discern Your will clearly.

**Images/Symbols/Numbers**                    **Interpretation/Discernment**

**Emotional Reflection:**

**Action Steps/Application:**

○
○
○
○
○

**Confirmation Notes (Follow Up):**

# AWAKENED WITH PURPOSE

*Every dream is personal — seek God's Word and the Holy Spirit for confirmation.*

**Date:**                **Time:**                **Dream Title:**

**Dream Description**                                          **Scriptural Connection**

### Prayer of Revelation
Lord, reveal what You are saying through this dream. Help me to walk in obedience and discern Your will clearly.

**Images/Symbols/Numbers**                          **Interpretation/Discernment**

**Emotional Reflection:**

**Action Steps/Application:**

○
○
○
○
○

**Confirmation Notes (Follow Up):**

# AWAKENED WITH PURPOSE

*Every dream is personal — seek God's Word and the Holy Spirit for confirmation.*

Date:                    Time:                    Dream Title:

**Dream Description**

**Scriptural Connection**

**Prayer of Revelation**

Lord, reveal what You are saying through this dream. Help me to walk in obedience and discern Your will clearly.

**Images/Symbols/Numbers**

**Interpretation/Discernment**

**Emotional Reflection:**

**Action Steps/Application:**
- ○
- ○
- ○
- ○
- ○

**Confirmation Notes (Follow Up):**

# AWAKENED WITH PURPOSE

*Every dream is personal — seek God's Word and the Holy Spirit for confirmation.*

**Date:**          **Time:**          **Dream Title:**

**Dream Description**

**Scriptural Connection**

**Prayer of Revelation**
Lord, reveal what You are saying through this dream. Help me to walk in obedience and discern Your will clearly.

**Images/Symbols/Numbers**

**Interpretation/Discernment**

**Emotional Reflection:**

**Action Steps/Application:**
- ◯
- ◯
- ◯
- ◯
- ◯

**Confirmation Notes (Follow Up):**

# AWAKENED WITH PURPOSE

*Every dream is personal — seek God's Word and the Holy Spirit for confirmation.*

**Date:**          **Time:**          **Dream Title:**

**Dream Description**

**Scriptural Connection**

### Prayer of Revelation
Lord, reveal what You are saying through this dream. Help me to walk in obedience and discern Your will clearly.

**Images/Symbols/Numbers**

**Interpretation/Discernment**

**Emotional Reflection:**

**Action Steps/Application:**
- ○
- ○
- ○
- ○
- ○

**Confirmation Notes (Follow Up):**

# AWAKENED WITH PURPOSE

*Every dream is personal — seek God's Word and the Holy Spirit for confirmation.*

**Date:**                **Time:**                **Dream Title:**

**Dream Description**

**Scriptural Connection**

### Prayer of Revelation
Lord, reveal what You are saying through this dream. Help me to walk in obedience and discern Your will clearly.

**Images/Symbols/Numbers**

**Interpretation/Discernment**

**Emotional Reflection:**

**Action Steps/Application:**
- ○
- ○
- ○
- ○
- ○

**Confirmation Notes (Follow Up):**

# AWAKENED WITH PURPOSE

*Every dream is personal — seek God's Word and the Holy Spirit for confirmation.*

Date:                Time:                Dream Title:

**Dream Description**

**Scriptural Connection**

**Prayer of Revelation**

Lord, reveal what You are saying through this dream. Help me to walk in obedience and discern Your will clearly.

**Images/Symbols/Numbers**

**Interpretation/Discernment**

**Emotional Reflection:**

**Action Steps/Application:**
- ○
- ○
- ○
- ○
- ○

**Confirmation Notes (Follow Up):**

# AWAKENED WITH PURPOSE

*Every dream is personal — seek God's Word and the Holy Spirit for confirmation.*

**Date:**      **Time:**      **Dream Title:**

**Dream Description**

**Scriptural Connection**

**Prayer of Revelation**
Lord, reveal what You are saying through this dream. Help me to walk in obedience and discern Your will clearly.

**Images/Symbols/Numbers**

**Interpretation/Discernment**

**Emotional Reflection:**

**Action Steps/Application:**
- ○
- ○
- ○
- ○
- ○

**Confirmation Notes (Follow Up):**

# AWAKENED WITH PURPOSE

*Every dream is personal — seek God's Word and the Holy Spirit for confirmation.*

**Date:**                **Time:**                **Dream Title:**

**Dream Description**

**Scriptural Connection**

**Prayer of Revelation**
Lord, reveal what You are saying through this dream. Help me to walk in obedience and discern Your will clearly.

**Images/Symbols/Numbers**

**Interpretation/Discernment**

**Emotional Reflection:**

**Action Steps/Application:**
- ○
- ○
- ○
- ○
- ○

**Confirmation Notes (Follow Up):**

# AWAKENED WITH PURPOSE

*Every dream is personal — seek God's Word and the Holy Spirit for confirmation.*

**Date:**                    **Time:**                    **Dream Title:**

**Dream Description**                    **Scriptural Connection**

**Prayer of Revelation**
Lord, reveal what You are saying through this dream. Help me to walk in obedience and discern Your will clearly.

**Images/Symbols/Numbers**                    **Interpretation/Discernment**

**Emotional Reflection:**

**Action Steps/Application:**
○
○
○
○
○

**Confirmation Notes (Follow Up):**

# AWAKENED WITH PURPOSE

*Every dream is personal — seek God's Word and the Holy Spirit for confirmation.*

Date:                Time:                Dream Title:

**Dream Description**

**Scriptural Connection**

**Prayer of Revelation**

Lord, reveal what You are saying through this dream. Help me to walk in obedience and discern Your will clearly.

**Images/Symbols/Numbers**

**Interpretation/Discernment**

**Emotional Reflection:**

**Action Steps/Application:**
- ○
- ○
- ○
- ○
- ○

**Confirmation Notes (Follow Up):**

# AWAKENED WITH PURPOSE

*Every dream is personal — seek God's Word and the Holy Spirit for confirmation.*

**Date:**          **Time:**          **Dream Title:**

**Dream Description**

**Scriptural Connection**

**Prayer of Revelation**
Lord, reveal what You are saying through this dream. Help me to walk in obedience and discern Your will clearly.

**Images/Symbols/Numbers**

**Interpretation/Discernment**

**Emotional Reflection:**

**Action Steps/Application:**
- ○
- ○
- ○
- ○
- ○

**Confirmation Notes (Follow Up):**

# AWAKENED WITH PURPOSE

*Every dream is personal — seek God's Word and the Holy Spirit for confirmation.*

Date:                    Time:                    Dream Title:

**Dream Description**

**Scriptural Connection**

**Prayer of Revelation**

Lord, reveal what You are saying through this dream. Help me to walk in obedience and discern Your will clearly.

**Images/Symbols/Numbers**

**Interpretation/Discernment**

**Emotional Reflection:**

**Action Steps/Application:**

○
○
○
○
○

**Confirmation Notes (Follow Up):**

# AWAKENED WITH PURPOSE

*Every dream is personal — seek God's Word and the Holy Spirit for confirmation.*

**Date:**　　　　　**Time:**　　　　　**Dream Title:**

**Dream Description**

**Scriptural Connection**

**Prayer of Revelation**

Lord, reveal what You are saying through this dream. Help me to walk in obedience and discern Your will clearly.

**Images/Symbols/Numbers**

**Interpretation/Discernment**

**Emotional Reflection:**

**Action Steps/Application:**
- ○
- ○
- ○
- ○
- ○

**Confirmation Notes (Follow Up):**

# AWAKENED WITH PURPOSE

*Every dream is personal — seek God's Word and the Holy Spirit for confirmation.*

**Date:** **Time:** **Dream Title:**

**Dream Description**

**Scriptural Connection**

**Prayer of Revelation**
Lord, reveal what You are saying through this dream. Help me to walk in obedience and discern Your will clearly.

**Images/Symbols/Numbers**

**Interpretation/Discernment**

**Emotional Reflection:**

**Action Steps/Application:**
- ○
- ○
- ○
- ○
- ○

**Confirmation Notes (Follow Up):**

# AWAKENED WITH PURPOSE

*Every dream is personal — seek God's Word and the Holy Spirit for confirmation.*

**Date:**            **Time:**            **Dream Title:**

**Dream Description**

**Scriptural Connection**

**Prayer of Revelation**
Lord, reveal what You are saying through this dream. Help me to walk in obedience and discern Your will clearly.

**Images/Symbols/Numbers**

**Interpretation/Discernment**

**Emotional Reflection:**

**Action Steps/Application:**
- ○
- ○
- ○
- ○
- ○

**Confirmation Notes (Follow Up):**

# AWAKENED WITH PURPOSE

*Every dream is personal — seek God's Word and the Holy Spirit for confirmation.*

**Date:**      **Time:**      **Dream Title:**

**Dream Description**

**Scriptural Connection**

**Prayer of Revelation**

Lord, reveal what You are saying through this dream. Help me to walk in obedience and discern Your will clearly.

**Images/Symbols/Numbers**

**Interpretation/Discernment**

**Emotional Reflection:**

**Action Steps/Application:**
- ◯
- ◯
- ◯
- ◯
- ◯

**Confirmation Notes (Follow Up):**

# AWAKENED WITH PURPOSE

*Every dream is personal — seek God's Word and the Holy Spirit for confirmation.*

**Date:**                    **Time:**                    **Dream Title:**

**Dream Description**                                              **Scriptural Connection**

**Prayer of Revelation**

Lord, reveal what You are saying through this dream. Help me to walk in obedience and discern Your will clearly.

**Images/Symbols/Numbers**                              **Interpretation/Discernment**

**Emotional Reflection:**

**Action Steps/Application:**
- ◯
- ◯
- ◯
- ◯
- ◯

**Confirmation Notes (Follow Up):**

# AWAKENED WITH PURPOSE

*Every dream is personal — seek God's Word and the Holy Spirit for confirmation.*

Date:                    Time:                    Dream Title:

**Dream Description**

**Scriptural Connection**

**Prayer of Revelation**

Lord, reveal what You are saying through this dream. Help me to walk in obedience and discern Your will clearly.

**Images/Symbols/Numbers**

**Interpretation/Discernment**

**Emotional Reflection:**

**Action Steps/Application:**

- ◯
- ◯
- ◯
- ◯
- ◯

**Confirmation Notes (Follow Up):**

# AWAKENED WITH PURPOSE

*Every dream is personal — seek God's Word and the Holy Spirit for confirmation.*

Date:                    Time:                    Dream Title:

**Dream Description**

**Scriptural Connection**

**Prayer of Revelation**

Lord, reveal what You are saying through this dream. Help me to walk in obedience and discern Your will clearly.

**Images/Symbols/Numbers**

**Interpretation/Discernment**

**Emotional Reflection:**

**Action Steps/Application:**

○
○
○
○
○

**Confirmation Notes (Follow Up):**

# AWAKENED WITH PURPOSE

*Every dream is personal — seek God's Word and the Holy Spirit for confirmation.*

**Date:**                **Time:**                **Dream Title:**

**Dream Description**

**Scriptural Connection**

**Prayer of Revelation**

Lord, reveal what You are saying through this dream. Help me to walk in obedience and discern Your will clearly.

**Images/Symbols/Numbers**

**Interpretation/Discernment**

**Emotional Reflection:**

**Action Steps/Application:**
- ○
- ○
- ○
- ○
- ○

**Confirmation Notes (Follow Up):**

# AWAKENED WITH PURPOSE

*Every dream is personal — seek God's Word and the Holy Spirit for confirmation.*

**Date:**          **Time:**          **Dream Title:**

**Dream Description**

**Scriptural Connection**

**Prayer of Revelation**

Lord, reveal what You are saying through this dream. Help me to walk in obedience and discern Your will clearly.

**Images/Symbols/Numbers**

**Interpretation/Discernment**

**Emotional Reflection:**

**Action Steps/Application:**
- ○
- ○
- ○
- ○
- ○

**Confirmation Notes (Follow Up):**

# AWAKENED WITH PURPOSE

*Every dream is personal — seek God's Word and the Holy Spirit for confirmation.*

**Date:**                **Time:**                **Dream Title:**

**Dream Description**                                                    **Scriptural Connection**

**Prayer of Revelation**

Lord, reveal what You are saying through this dream. Help me to walk in obedience and discern Your will clearly.

**Images/Symbols/Numbers**                                    **Interpretation/Discernment**

**Emotional Reflection:**

**Action Steps/Application:**

○
○
○
○
○

**Confirmation Notes (Follow Up):**

# AWAKENED WITH PURPOSE

*Every dream is personal — seek God's Word and the Holy Spirit for confirmation.*

**Date:**      **Time:**      **Dream Title:**

**Dream Description**

**Scriptural Connection**

**Prayer of Revelation**

Lord, reveal what You are saying through this dream. Help me to walk in obedience and discern Your will clearly.

**Images/Symbols/Numbers**

**Interpretation/Discernment**

**Emotional Reflection:**

**Action Steps/Application:**
- ○
- ○
- ○
- ○
- ○

**Confirmation Notes (Follow Up):**

# AWAKENED WITH PURPOSE

*Every dream is personal — seek God's Word and the Holy Spirit for confirmation.*

Date:                    Time:                    Dream Title:

**Dream Description**

**Scriptural Connection**

**Prayer of Revelation**
Lord, reveal what You are saying through this dream. Help me to walk in obedience and discern Your will clearly.

**Images/Symbols/Numbers**

**Interpretation/Discernment**

**Emotional Reflection:**

**Action Steps/Application:**
- ◯
- ◯
- ◯
- ◯
- ◯

**Confirmation Notes (Follow Up):**

# AWAKENED WITH PURPOSE

*Every dream is personal — seek God's Word and the Holy Spirit for confirmation.*

**Date:**                **Time:**                **Dream Title:**

**Dream Description**

**Scriptural Connection**

**Prayer of Revelation**

Lord, reveal what You are saying through this dream. Help me to walk in obedience and discern Your will clearly.

**Images/Symbols/Numbers**

**Interpretation/Discernment**

**Emotional Reflection:**

**Action Steps/Application:**
- ○
- ○
- ○
- ○
- ○

**Confirmation Notes (Follow Up):**

# AWAKENED WITH PURPOSE

*Every dream is personal — seek God's Word and the Holy Spirit for confirmation.*

Date:                Time:                Dream Title:

**Dream Description**

**Scriptural Connection**

**Prayer of Revelation**

Lord, reveal what You are saying through this dream. Help me to walk in obedience and discern Your will clearly.

**Images/Symbols/Numbers**

**Interpretation/Discernment**

**Emotional Reflection:**

**Action Steps/Application:**

○
○
○
○
○

**Confirmation Notes (Follow Up):**

# AWAKENED WITH PURPOSE

*Every dream is personal — seek God's Word and the Holy Spirit for confirmation.*

**Date:**                **Time:**                **Dream Title:**

**Dream Description**

**Scriptural Connection**

**Prayer of Revelation**
Lord, reveal what You are saying through this dream. Help me to walk in obedience and discern Your will clearly.

**Images/Symbols/Numbers**

**Interpretation/Discernment**

**Emotional Reflection:**

**Action Steps/Application:**
- ○
- ○
- ○
- ○
- ○

**Confirmation Notes (Follow Up):**

# AWAKENED WITH PURPOSE

*Every dream is personal — seek God's Word and the Holy Spirit for confirmation.*

Date:                Time:                Dream Title:

**Dream Description**

**Scriptural Connection**

**Prayer of Revelation**
Lord, reveal what You are saying through this dream. Help me to walk in obedience and discern Your will clearly.

**Images/Symbols/Numbers**

**Interpretation/Discernment**

**Emotional Reflection:**

**Action Steps/Application:**
- ○
- ○
- ○
- ○
- ○

**Confirmation Notes (Follow Up):**

# AWAKENED WITH PURPOSE

*Every dream is personal — seek God's Word and the Holy Spirit for confirmation.*

**Date:**                **Time:**                **Dream Title:**

**Dream Description**

**Scriptural Connection**

**Prayer of Revelation**

Lord, reveal what You are saying through this dream. Help me to walk in obedience and discern Your will clearly.

**Images/Symbols/Numbers**

**Interpretation/Discernment**

**Emotional Reflection:**

**Action Steps/Application:**

○
○
○
○
○

**Confirmation Notes (Follow Up):**

# AWAKENED WITH PURPOSE

*Every dream is personal — seek God's Word and the Holy Spirit for confirmation.*

**Date:**                **Time:**                **Dream Title:**

**Dream Description**

**Scriptural Connection**

**Prayer of Revelation**

Lord, reveal what You are saying through this dream. Help me to walk in obedience and discern Your will clearly.

**Images/Symbols/Numbers**

**Interpretation/Discernment**

**Emotional Reflection:**

**Action Steps/Application:**
- ○
- ○
- ○
- ○
- ○

**Confirmation Notes (Follow Up):**

# AWAKENED WITH PURPOSE

*Every dream is personal — seek God's Word and the Holy Spirit for confirmation.*

Date:                Time:                Dream Title:

**Dream Description**

**Scriptural Connection**

**Prayer of Revelation**

Lord, reveal what You are saying through this dream. Help me to walk in obedience and discern Your will clearly.

**Images/Symbols/Numbers**

**Interpretation/Discernment**

**Emotional Reflection:**

**Action Steps/Application:**
- ○
- ○
- ○
- ○
- ○

**Confirmation Notes (Follow Up):**

# AWAKENED WITH PURPOSE

*Every dream is personal — seek God's Word and the Holy Spirit for confirmation.*

**Date:**                **Time:**                **Dream Title:**

**Dream Description**                                          **Scriptural Connection**

**Prayer of Revelation**
Lord, reveal what You are saying through this dream. Help me to walk in obedience and discern Your will clearly.

**Images/Symbols/Numbers**                          **Interpretation/Discernment**

**Emotional Reflection:**

**Action Steps/Application:**

○
○
○
○
○

**Confirmation Notes (Follow Up):**

# AWAKENED WITH PURPOSE

*Every dream is personal — seek God's Word and the Holy Spirit for confirmation.*

**Date:**     **Time:**     **Dream Title:**

**Dream Description**

**Scriptural Connection**

### Prayer of Revelation
Lord, reveal what You are saying through this dream. Help me to walk in obedience and discern Your will clearly.

**Images/Symbols/Numbers**

**Interpretation/Discernment**

**Emotional Reflection:**

**Action Steps/Application:**
- ◯
- ◯
- ◯
- ◯
- ◯

**Confirmation Notes (Follow Up):**

# AWAKENED WITH PURPOSE

*Every dream is personal — seek God's Word and the Holy Spirit for confirmation.*

**Date:**             **Time:**             **Dream Title:**

**Dream Description**

**Scriptural Connection**

**Prayer of Revelation**

Lord, reveal what You are saying through this dream. Help me to walk in obedience and discern Your will clearly.

**Images/Symbols/Numbers**

**Interpretation/Discernment**

**Emotional Reflection:**

**Action Steps/Application:**

○
○
○
○
○

**Confirmation Notes (Follow Up):**

# AWAKENED WITH PURPOSE

*Every dream is personal — seek God's Word and the Holy Spirit for confirmation.*

**Date:**      **Time:**      **Dream Title:**

**Dream Description**

**Scriptural Connection**

### Prayer of Revelation
Lord, reveal what You are saying through this dream. Help me to walk in obedience and discern Your will clearly.

**Images/Symbols/Numbers**

**Interpretation/Discernment**

**Emotional Reflection:**

**Action Steps/Application:**
- ○
- ○
- ○
- ○
- ○

**Confirmation Notes (Follow Up):**

# AWAKENED WITH PURPOSE

*Every dream is personal — seek God's Word and the Holy Spirit for confirmation.*

Date:                    Time:                    Dream Title:

**Dream Description**

**Scriptural Connection**

**Prayer of Revelation**
Lord, reveal what You are saying through this dream. Help me to walk in obedience and discern Your will clearly.

**Images/Symbols/Numbers**

**Interpretation/Discernment**

**Emotional Reflection:**

**Action Steps/Application:**
○
○
○
○
○

**Confirmation Notes (Follow Up):**

# AWAKENED WITH PURPOSE

*Every dream is personal — seek God's Word and the Holy Spirit for confirmation.*

**Date:**          **Time:**          **Dream Title:**

**Dream Description**

**Scriptural Connection**

**Prayer of Revelation**
Lord, reveal what You are saying through this dream. Help me to walk in obedience and discern Your will clearly.

**Images/Symbols/Numbers**

**Interpretation/Discernment**

**Emotional Reflection:**

**Action Steps/Application:**
- ◯
- ◯
- ◯
- ◯
- ◯

**Confirmation Notes (Follow Up):**

# AWAKENED WITH PURPOSE

*Every dream is personal — seek God's Word and the Holy Spirit for confirmation.*

**Date:**                **Time:**                **Dream Title:**

**Dream Description**

**Scriptural Connection**

**Prayer of Revelation**
Lord, reveal what You are saying through this dream. Help me to walk in obedience and discern Your will clearly.

**Images/Symbols/Numbers**

**Interpretation/Discernment**

**Emotional Reflection:**

**Action Steps/Application:**
- ○
- ○
- ○
- ○
- ○

**Confirmation Notes (Follow Up):**

# AWAKENED WITH PURPOSE

*Every dream is personal — seek God's Word and the Holy Spirit for confirmation.*

**Date:**             **Time:**             **Dream Title:**

**Dream Description**                                          **Scriptural Connection**

**Prayer of Revelation**

Lord, reveal what You are saying through this dream. Help me to walk in obedience and discern Your will clearly.

**Images/Symbols/Numbers**                          **Interpretation/Discernment**

**Emotional Reflection:**

**Action Steps/Application:**
- ○
- ○
- ○
- ○
- ○

**Confirmation Notes (Follow Up):**

# AWAKENED WITH PURPOSE

*Every dream is personal — seek God's Word and the Holy Spirit for confirmation.*

Date:                Time:                Dream Title:

**Dream Description**

**Scriptural Connection**

**Prayer of Revelation**

Lord, reveal what You are saying through this dream. Help me to walk in obedience and discern Your will clearly.

**Images/Symbols/Numbers**

**Interpretation/Discernment**

**Emotional Reflection:**

**Action Steps/Application:**
- ◯
- ◯
- ◯
- ◯
- ◯

**Confirmation Notes (Follow Up):**

# AWAKENED WITH PURPOSE

*Every dream is personal — seek God's Word and the Holy Spirit for confirmation.*

**Date:**  **Time:**  **Dream Title:**

**Dream Description**

**Scriptural Connection**

**Prayer of Revelation**
Lord, reveal what You are saying through this dream. Help me to walk in obedience and discern Your will clearly.

**Images/Symbols/Numbers**

**Interpretation/Discernment**

**Emotional Reflection:**

**Action Steps/Application:**
- ○
- ○
- ○
- ○
- ○

**Confirmation Notes (Follow Up):**

# AWAKENED WITH PURPOSE

*Every dream is personal — seek God's Word and the Holy Spirit for confirmation.*

Date:                    Time:                    Dream Title:

**Dream Description**

**Scriptural Connection**

**Prayer of Revelation**

Lord, reveal what You are saying through this dream. Help me to walk in obedience and discern Your will clearly.

**Images/Symbols/Numbers**

**Interpretation/Discernment**

**Emotional Reflection:**

**Action Steps/Application:**

○
○
○
○
○

**Confirmation Notes (Follow Up):**

# AWAKENED WITH PURPOSE

*Every dream is personal — seek God's Word and the Holy Spirit for confirmation.*

**Date:**                    **Time:**                    **Dream Title:**

**Dream Description**

**Scriptural Connection**

**Prayer of Revelation**
Lord, reveal what You are saying through this dream. Help me to walk in obedience and discern Your will clearly.

**Images/Symbols/Numbers**

**Interpretation/Discernment**

**Emotional Reflection:**

**Action Steps/Application:**
- ○
- ○
- ○
- ○
- ○

**Confirmation Notes (Follow Up):**

# AWAKENED WITH PURPOSE

*Every dream is personal — seek God's Word and the Holy Spirit for confirmation.*

**Date:**                **Time:**                **Dream Title:**

**Dream Description**

**Scriptural Connection**

**Prayer of Revelation**

Lord, reveal what You are saying through this dream. Help me to walk in obedience and discern Your will clearly.

**Images/Symbols/Numbers**

**Interpretation/Discernment**

**Emotional Reflection:**

**Action Steps/Application:**
- ◯
- ◯
- ◯
- ◯
- ◯

**Confirmation Notes (Follow Up):**

# AWAKENED WITH PURPOSE

*Every dream is personal — seek God's Word and the Holy Spirit for confirmation.*

**Date:**          **Time:**          **Dream Title:**

**Dream Description**

**Scriptural Connection**

**Prayer of Revelation**
Lord, reveal what You are saying through this dream. Help me to walk in obedience and discern Your will clearly.

**Images/Symbols/Numbers**

**Interpretation/Discernment**

**Emotional Reflection:**

**Action Steps/Application:**
- ○
- ○
- ○
- ○
- ○

**Confirmation Notes (Follow Up):**

# AWAKENED WITH PURPOSE

*Every dream is personal — seek God's Word and the Holy Spirit for confirmation.*

**Date:**          **Time:**          **Dream Title:**

**Dream Description**

**Scriptural Connection**

**Prayer of Revelation**

Lord, reveal what You are saying through this dream. Help me to walk in obedience and discern Your will clearly.

**Images/Symbols/Numbers**

**Interpretation/Discernment**

**Emotional Reflection:**

**Action Steps/Application:**

- ○
- ○
- ○
- ○
- ○

**Confirmation Notes (Follow Up):**

# AWAKENED WITH PURPOSE

*Every dream is personal — seek God's Word and the Holy Spirit for confirmation.*

**Date:**          **Time:**          **Dream Title:**

**Dream Description**

**Scriptural Connection**

### Prayer of Revelation
Lord, reveal what You are saying through this dream. Help me to walk in obedience and discern Your will clearly.

**Images/Symbols/Numbers**

**Interpretation/Discernment**

**Emotional Reflection:**

**Action Steps/Application:**
- ○
- ○
- ○
- ○
- ○

**Confirmation Notes (Follow Up):**

# AWAKENED WITH PURPOSE

*Every dream is personal — seek God's Word and the Holy Spirit for confirmation.*

**Date:**                **Time:**                **Dream Title:**

**Dream Description**

**Scriptural Connection**

### Prayer of Revelation

Lord, reveal what You are saying through this dream. Help me to walk in obedience and discern Your will clearly.

**Images/Symbols/Numbers**

**Interpretation/Discernment**

**Emotional Reflection:**

**Action Steps/Application:**

○
○
○
○
○

**Confirmation Notes (Follow Up):**

# AWAKENED WITH PURPOSE

*Every dream is personal — seek God's Word and the Holy Spirit for confirmation.*

Date:                Time:                Dream Title:

**Dream Description**

**Scriptural Connection**

**Prayer of Revelation**
Lord, reveal what You are saying through this dream. Help me to walk in obedience and discern Your will clearly.

**Images/Symbols/Numbers**

**Interpretation/Discernment**

**Emotional Reflection:**

**Action Steps/Application:**
- ○
- ○
- ○
- ○
- ○

**Confirmation Notes (Follow Up):**

# AWAKENED WITH PURPOSE

*Every dream is personal — seek God's Word and the Holy Spirit for confirmation.*

**Date:**      **Time:**      **Dream Title:**

**Dream Description**

**Scriptural Connection**

### Prayer of Revelation

Lord, reveal what You are saying through this dream. Help me to walk in obedience and discern Your will clearly.

**Images/Symbols/Numbers**

**Interpretation/Discernment**

**Emotional Reflection:**

**Action Steps/Application:**
- ○
- ○
- ○
- ○
- ○

**Confirmation Notes (Follow Up):**

# AWAKENED WITH PURPOSE

*Every dream is personal — seek God's Word and the Holy Spirit for confirmation.*

**Date:**      **Time:**      **Dream Title:**

**Dream Description**

**Scriptural Connection**

### Prayer of Revelation
Lord, reveal what You are saying through this dream. Help me to walk in obedience and discern Your will clearly.

**Images/Symbols/Numbers**

**Interpretation/Discernment**

**Emotional Reflection:**

**Action Steps/Application:**
- ○
- ○
- ○
- ○
- ○

**Confirmation Notes (Follow Up):**

# AWAKENED WITH PURPOSE

*Every dream is personal — seek God's Word and the Holy Spirit for confirmation.*

**Date:**                **Time:**                **Dream Title:**

**Dream Description**

**Scriptural Connection**

### Prayer of Revelation
Lord, reveal what You are saying through this dream. Help me to walk in obedience and discern Your will clearly.

**Images/Symbols/Numbers**

**Interpretation/Discernment**

**Emotional Reflection:**

**Action Steps/Application:**
- ○
- ○
- ○
- ○
- ○

**Confirmation Notes (Follow Up):**

# AWAKENED WITH PURPOSE

*Every dream is personal — seek God's Word and the Holy Spirit for confirmation.*

**Date:**                **Time:**                **Dream Title:**

**Dream Description**

**Scriptural Connection**

### Prayer of Revelation
Lord, reveal what You are saying through this dream. Help me to walk in obedience and discern Your will clearly.

**Images/Symbols/Numbers**

**Interpretation/Discernment**

**Emotional Reflection:**

**Action Steps/Application:**
- ○
- ○
- ○
- ○
- ○

**Confirmation Notes (Follow Up):**

# AWAKENED WITH PURPOSE

*Every dream is personal — seek God's Word and the Holy Spirit for confirmation.*

**Date:**                **Time:**                **Dream Title:**

**Dream Description**

**Scriptural Connection**

### Prayer of Revelation
Lord, reveal what You are saying through this dream. Help me to walk in obedience and discern Your will clearly.

**Images/Symbols/Numbers**

**Interpretation/Discernment**

**Emotional Reflection:**

**Action Steps/Application:**
- ○
- ○
- ○
- ○
- ○

**Confirmation Notes (Follow Up):**

# AWAKENED WITH PURPOSE

*Every dream is personal — seek God's Word and the Holy Spirit for confirmation.*

**Date:**           **Time:**           **Dream Title:**

**Dream Description**

**Scriptural Connection**

### Prayer of Revelation
Lord, reveal what You are saying through this dream. Help me to walk in obedience and discern Your will clearly.

**Images/Symbols/Numbers**

**Interpretation/Discernment**

**Emotional Reflection:**

**Action Steps/Application:**
- ◯
- ◯
- ◯
- ◯
- ◯

**Confirmation Notes (Follow Up):**

# AWAKENED WITH PURPOSE

*Every dream is personal — seek God's Word and the Holy Spirit for confirmation.*

**Date:**                    **Time:**                    **Dream Title:**

**Dream Description**

**Scriptural Connection**

**Prayer of Revelation**
Lord, reveal what You are saying through this dream. Help me to walk in obedience and discern Your will clearly.

**Images/Symbols/Numbers**

**Interpretation/Discernment**

**Emotional Reflection:**

**Action Steps/Application:**
- ○
- ○
- ○
- ○
- ○

**Confirmation Notes (Follow Up):**

# AWAKENED WITH PURPOSE

*Every dream is personal — seek God's Word and the Holy Spirit for confirmation.*

**Date:**                    **Time:**                    **Dream Title:**

**Dream Description**

**Scriptural Connection**

**Prayer of Revelation**
Lord, reveal what You are saying through this dream. Help me to walk in obedience and discern Your will clearly.

**Images/Symbols/Numbers**

**Interpretation/Discernment**

**Emotional Reflection:**

**Action Steps/Application:**
- ◯
- ◯
- ◯
- ◯
- ◯

**Confirmation Notes (Follow Up):**

# AWAKENED WITH PURPOSE

*Every dream is personal — seek God's Word and the Holy Spirit for confirmation.*

Date:                Time:                Dream Title:

**Dream Description**

**Scriptural Connection**

**Prayer of Revelation**

Lord, reveal what You are saying through this dream. Help me to walk in obedience and discern Your will clearly.

**Images/Symbols/Numbers**

**Interpretation/Discernment**

**Emotional Reflection:**

**Action Steps/Application:**

○
○
○
○
○

**Confirmation Notes (Follow Up):**

# AWAKENED WITH PURPOSE

*Every dream is personal — seek God's Word and the Holy Spirit for confirmation.*

**Date:**      **Time:**      **Dream Title:**

**Dream Description**

**Scriptural Connection**

**Prayer of Revelation**
Lord, reveal what You are saying through this dream. Help me to walk in obedience and discern Your will clearly.

**Images/Symbols/Numbers**

**Interpretation/Discernment**

**Emotional Reflection:**

**Action Steps/Application:**
- ◯
- ◯
- ◯
- ◯
- ◯

**Confirmation Notes (Follow Up):**

# AWAKENED WITH PURPOSE

*Every dream is personal — seek God's Word and the Holy Spirit for confirmation.*

**Date:**             **Time:**                 **Dream Title:**

**Dream Description**

**Scriptural Connection**

**Prayer of Revelation**

Lord, reveal what You are saying through this dream. Help me to walk in obedience and discern Your will clearly.

**Images/Symbols/Numbers**

**Interpretation/Discernment**

**Emotional Reflection:**

**Action Steps/Application:**

- ○
- ○
- ○
- ○
- ○

**Confirmation Notes (Follow Up):**

# AWAKENED WITH PURPOSE

*Every dream is personal — seek God's Word and the Holy Spirit for confirmation.*

**Date:**                **Time:**                **Dream Title:**

**Dream Description**

**Scriptural Connection**

**Prayer of Revelation**
Lord, reveal what You are saying through this dream. Help me to walk in obedience and discern Your will clearly.

**Images/Symbols/Numbers**

**Interpretation/Discernment**

**Emotional Reflection:**

**Action Steps/Application:**
- ○
- ○
- ○
- ○
- ○

**Confirmation Notes (Follow Up):**

# AWAKENED WITH PURPOSE

*Every dream is personal — seek God's Word and the Holy Spirit for confirmation.*

**Date:**            **Time:**            **Dream Title:**

**Dream Description**

**Scriptural Connection**

**Prayer of Revelation**
Lord, reveal what You are saying through this dream. Help me to walk in obedience and discern Your will clearly.

**Images/Symbols/Numbers**

**Interpretation/Discernment**

**Emotional Reflection:**

**Action Steps/Application:**
- ◯
- ◯
- ◯
- ◯
- ◯

**Confirmation Notes (Follow Up):**

# AWAKENED WITH PURPOSE

*Every dream is personal — seek God's Word and the Holy Spirit for confirmation.*

**Date:**      **Time:**      **Dream Title:**

**Dream Description**

**Scriptural Connection**

### Prayer of Revelation
Lord, reveal what You are saying through this dream. Help me to walk in obedience and discern Your will clearly.

**Images/Symbols/Numbers**

**Interpretation/Discernment**

**Emotional Reflection:**

**Action Steps/Application:**
- ◯
- ◯
- ◯
- ◯
- ◯

**Confirmation Notes (Follow Up):**

# AWAKENED WITH PURPOSE

*Every dream is personal — seek God's Word and the Holy Spirit for confirmation.*

**Date:**      **Time:**      **Dream Title:**

**Dream Description**

**Scriptural Connection**

**Prayer of Revelation**

Lord, reveal what You are saying through this dream. Help me to walk in obedience and discern Your will clearly.

**Images/Symbols/Numbers**

**Interpretation/Discernment**

**Emotional Reflection:**

**Action Steps/Application:**

- ◯
- ◯
- ◯
- ◯
- ◯

**Confirmation Notes (Follow Up):**

# AWAKENED WITH PURPOSE

*Every dream is personal — seek God's Word and the Holy Spirit for confirmation.*

**Date:**            **Time:**            **Dream Title:**

**Dream Description**

**Scriptural Connection**

**Prayer of Revelation**
Lord, reveal what You are saying through this dream. Help me to walk in obedience and discern Your will clearly.

**Images/Symbols/Numbers**

**Interpretation/Discernment**

**Emotional Reflection:**

**Action Steps/Application:**
- ○
- ○
- ○
- ○
- ○

**Confirmation Notes (Follow Up):**

# AWAKENED WITH PURPOSE

*Every dream is personal — seek God's Word and the Holy Spirit for confirmation.*

**Date:**                    **Time:**                    **Dream Title:**

**Dream Description**

**Scriptural Connection**

### Prayer of Revelation

Lord, reveal what You are saying through this dream. Help me to walk in obedience and discern Your will clearly.

**Images/Symbols/Numbers**

**Interpretation/Discernment**

**Emotional Reflection:**

**Action Steps/Application:**
- ○
- ○
- ○
- ○
- ○

**Confirmation Notes (Follow Up):**

# AWAKENED WITH PURPOSE

*Every dream is personal — seek God's Word and the Holy Spirit for confirmation.*

**Date:**　　　　　**Time:**　　　　　**Dream Title:**

**Dream Description**

**Scriptural Connection**

**Prayer of Revelation**
Lord, reveal what You are saying through this dream. Help me to walk in obedience and discern Your will clearly.

**Images/Symbols/Numbers**

**Interpretation/Discernment**

**Emotional Reflection:**

**Action Steps/Application:**
- ○
- ○
- ○
- ○
- ○

**Confirmation Notes (Follow Up):**

# AWAKENED WITH PURPOSE

*Every dream is personal — seek God's Word and the Holy Spirit for confirmation.*

**Date:**        **Time:**        **Dream Title:**

**Dream Description**

**Scriptural Connection**

### Prayer of Revelation
Lord, reveal what You are saying through this dream. Help me to walk in obedience and discern Your will clearly.

**Images/Symbols/Numbers**

**Interpretation/Discernment**

**Emotional Reflection:**

**Action Steps/Application:**
- ◯
- ◯
- ◯
- ◯
- ◯

**Confirmation Notes (Follow Up):**

# AWAKENED WITH PURPOSE

*Every dream is personal — seek God's Word and the Holy Spirit for confirmation.*

**Date:**　　　　　**Time:**　　　　　**Dream Title:**

**Dream Description**

**Scriptural Connection**

**Prayer of Revelation**
Lord, reveal what You are saying through this dream. Help me to walk in obedience and discern Your will clearly.

**Images/Symbols/Numbers**

**Interpretation/Discernment**

**Emotional Reflection:**

**Action Steps/Application:**
- ○
- ○
- ○
- ○
- ○

**Confirmation Notes (Follow Up):**

# AWAKENED WITH PURPOSE

*Every dream is personal — seek God's Word and the Holy Spirit for confirmation.*

**Date:**      **Time:**      **Dream Title:**

**Dream Description**

**Scriptural Connection**

### Prayer of Revelation
Lord, reveal what You are saying through this dream. Help me to walk in obedience and discern Your will clearly.

**Images/Symbols/Numbers**

**Interpretation/Discernment**

**Emotional Reflection:**

**Action Steps/Application:**
- ○
- ○
- ○
- ○
- ○

**Confirmation Notes (Follow Up):**

# AWAKENED WITH PURPOSE

*Every dream is personal — seek God's Word and the Holy Spirit for confirmation.*

**Date:**        **Time:**        **Dream Title:**

**Dream Description**

**Scriptural Connection**

**Prayer of Revelation**

Lord, reveal what You are saying through this dream. Help me to walk in obedience and discern Your will clearly.

**Images/Symbols/Numbers**

**Interpretation/Discernment**

**Emotional Reflection:**

**Action Steps/Application:**
- ◯
- ◯
- ◯
- ◯
- ◯

**Confirmation Notes (Follow Up):**

# AWAKENED WITH PURPOSE

*Every dream is personal — seek God's Word and the Holy Spirit for confirmation.*

**Date:**                **Time:**                **Dream Title:**

**Dream Description**

**Scriptural Connection**

### Prayer of Revelation

Lord, reveal what You are saying through this dream. Help me to walk in obedience and discern Your will clearly.

**Images/Symbols/Numbers**

**Interpretation/Discernment**

**Emotional Reflection:**

**Action Steps/Application:**
- ○
- ○
- ○
- ○
- ○

**Confirmation Notes (Follow Up):**

# AWAKENED WITH PURPOSE

*Every dream is personal — seek God's Word and the Holy Spirit for confirmation.*

**Date:**          **Time:**          **Dream Title:**

**Dream Description**

**Scriptural Connection**

**Prayer of Revelation**
Lord, reveal what You are saying through this dream. Help me to walk in obedience and discern Your will clearly.

**Images/Symbols/Numbers**

**Interpretation/Discernment**

**Emotional Reflection:**

**Action Steps/Application:**
○
○
○
○
○

**Confirmation Notes (Follow Up):**

# AWAKENED WITH PURPOSE

*Every dream is personal — seek God's Word and the Holy Spirit for confirmation.*

**Date:**                **Time:**                **Dream Title:**

**Dream Description**                                          **Scriptural Connection**

**Prayer of Revelation**

Lord, reveal what You are saying through this dream. Help me to walk in obedience and discern Your will clearly.

**Images/Symbols/Numbers**                            **Interpretation/Discernment**

**Emotional Reflection:**

**Action Steps/Application:**                         **Confirmation Notes (Follow Up):**

○

○

○

○

○

# AWAKENED WITH PURPOSE

*Every dream is personal — seek God's Word and the Holy Spirit for confirmation.*

**Date:**        **Time:**        **Dream Title:**

**Dream Description**

**Scriptural Connection**

### Prayer of Revelation

Lord, reveal what You are saying through this dream. Help me to walk in obedience and discern Your will clearly.

**Images/Symbols/Numbers**

**Interpretation/Discernment**

**Emotional Reflection:**

**Action Steps/Application:**
- ○
- ○
- ○
- ○
- ○

**Confirmation Notes (Follow Up):**

# AWAKENED WITH PURPOSE

*Every dream is personal — seek God's Word and the Holy Spirit for confirmation.*

**Date:**                **Time:**                **Dream Title:**

**Dream Description**

**Scriptural Connection**

### Prayer of Revelation

Lord, reveal what You are saying through this dream. Help me to walk in obedience and discern Your will clearly.

**Images/Symbols/Numbers**

**Interpretation/Discernment**

**Emotional Reflection:**

**Action Steps/Application:**

- ◯
- ◯
- ◯
- ◯
- ◯

**Confirmation Notes (Follow Up):**

# AWAKENED WITH PURPOSE

*Every dream is personal — seek God's Word and the Holy Spirit for confirmation.*

**Date:** **Time:** **Dream Title:**

**Dream Description**

**Scriptural Connection**

**Prayer of Revelation**

Lord, reveal what You are saying through this dream. Help me to walk in obedience and discern Your will clearly.

**Images/Symbols/Numbers**

**Interpretation/Discernment**

**Emotional Reflection:**

**Action Steps/Application:**
- ○
- ○
- ○
- ○
- ○

**Confirmation Notes (Follow Up):**

# AWAKENED WITH PURPOSE

*Every dream is personal — seek God's Word and the Holy Spirit for confirmation.*

**Date:** **Time:** **Dream Title:**

**Dream Description**

**Scriptural Connection**

**Prayer of Revelation**

Lord, reveal what You are saying through this dream. Help me to walk in obedience and discern Your will clearly.

**Images/Symbols/Numbers**

**Interpretation/Discernment**

**Emotional Reflection:**

**Action Steps/Application:**
- ◯
- ◯
- ◯
- ◯
- ◯

**Confirmation Notes (Follow Up):**

# AWAKENED WITH PURPOSE

*Every dream is personal — seek God's Word and the Holy Spirit for confirmation.*

**Date:**                    **Time:**                    **Dream Title:**

**Dream Description**                                    **Scriptural Connection**

### Prayer of Revelation
Lord, reveal what You are saying through this dream. Help me to walk in obedience and discern Your will clearly.

**Images/Symbols/Numbers**                              **Interpretation/Discernment**

**Emotional Reflection:**

**Action Steps/Application:**
- ◯
- ◯
- ◯
- ◯
- ◯

**Confirmation Notes (Follow Up):**

# AWAKENED WITH PURPOSE

*Every dream is personal — seek God's Word and the Holy Spirit for confirmation.*

Date:                    Time:                    Dream Title:

**Dream Description**

**Scriptural Connection**

**Prayer of Revelation**

Lord, reveal what You are saying through this dream. Help me to walk in obedience and discern Your will clearly.

**Images/Symbols/Numbers**

**Interpretation/Discernment**

**Emotional Reflection:**

**Action Steps/Application:**

○
○
○
○
○

**Confirmation Notes (Follow Up):**

# AWAKENED WITH PURPOSE

*Every dream is personal — seek God's Word and the Holy Spirit for confirmation.*

**Date:**                    **Time:**                    **Dream Title:**

**Dream Description**

**Scriptural Connection**

**Prayer of Revelation**

Lord, reveal what You are saying through this dream. Help me to walk in obedience and discern Your will clearly.

**Images/Symbols/Numbers**

**Interpretation/Discernment**

**Emotional Reflection:**

**Action Steps/Application:**
- ○
- ○
- ○
- ○
- ○

**Confirmation Notes (Follow Up):**

# AWAKENED WITH PURPOSE

*Every dream is personal — seek God's Word and the Holy Spirit for confirmation.*

**Date:**      **Time:**      **Dream Title:**

**Dream Description**

**Scriptural Connection**

### Prayer of Revelation
Lord, reveal what You are saying through this dream. Help me to walk in obedience and discern Your will clearly.

**Images/Symbols/Numbers**

**Interpretation/Discernment**

**Emotional Reflection:**

**Action Steps/Application:**
- ◯
- ◯
- ◯
- ◯
- ◯

**Confirmation Notes (Follow Up):**

# AWAKENED WITH PURPOSE

*Every dream is personal — seek God's Word and the Holy Spirit for confirmation.*

**Date:**                **Time:**                **Dream Title:**

**Dream Description**

**Scriptural Connection**

**Prayer of Revelation**
Lord, reveal what You are saying through this dream. Help me to walk in obedience and discern Your will clearly.

**Images/Symbols/Numbers**

**Interpretation/Discernment**

**Emotional Reflection:**

**Action Steps/Application:**
- ○
- ○
- ○
- ○
- ○

**Confirmation Notes (Follow Up):**

# AWAKENED WITH PURPOSE

*Every dream is personal — seek God's Word and the Holy Spirit for confirmation.*

Date:                    Time:                    Dream Title:

**Dream Description**

**Scriptural Connection**

**Prayer of Revelation**

Lord, reveal what You are saying through this dream. Help me to walk in obedience and discern Your will clearly.

**Images/Symbols/Numbers**

**Interpretation/Discernment**

**Emotional Reflection:**

**Action Steps/Application:**
- ○
- ○
- ○
- ○
- ○

**Confirmation Notes (Follow Up):**

# AWAKENED WITH PURPOSE

*Every dream is personal — seek God's Word and the Holy Spirit for confirmation.*

**Date:**                **Time:**                **Dream Title:**

**Dream Description**

**Scriptural Connection**

**Prayer of Revelation**

Lord, reveal what You are saying through this dream. Help me to walk in obedience and discern Your will clearly.

**Images/Symbols/Numbers**

**Interpretation/Discernment**

**Emotional Reflection:**

**Action Steps/Application:**

○
○
○
○
○

**Confirmation Notes (Follow Up):**

# AWAKENED WITH PURPOSE

*Every dream is personal — seek God's Word and the Holy Spirit for confirmation.*

**Date:**                **Time:**                **Dream Title:**

**Dream Description**

**Scriptural Connection**

**Prayer of Revelation**

Lord, reveal what You are saying through this dream. Help me to walk in obedience and discern Your will clearly.

**Images/Symbols/Numbers**

**Interpretation/Discernment**

**Emotional Reflection:**

**Action Steps/Application:**

○
○
○
○
○

**Confirmation Notes (Follow Up):**

# AWAKENED WITH PURPOSE

*Every dream is personal — seek God's Word and the Holy Spirit for confirmation.*

**Date:**                    **Time:**                    **Dream Title:**

**Dream Description**

**Scriptural Connection**

**Prayer of Revelation**
Lord, reveal what You are saying through this dream. Help me to walk in obedience and discern Your will clearly.

**Images/Symbols/Numbers**

**Interpretation/Discernment**

**Emotional Reflection:**

**Action Steps/Application:**
○
○
○
○
○

**Confirmation Notes (Follow Up):**

# AWAKENED WITH PURPOSE

*Every dream is personal — seek God's Word and the Holy Spirit for confirmation.*

**Date:**          **Time:**          **Dream Title:**

**Dream Description**

**Scriptural Connection**

**Prayer of Revelation**

Lord, reveal what You are saying through this dream. Help me to walk in obedience and discern Your will clearly.

**Images/Symbols/Numbers**

**Interpretation/Discernment**

**Emotional Reflection:**

**Action Steps/Application:**

○
○
○
○
○

**Confirmation Notes (Follow Up):**

# AWAKENED WITH PURPOSE

*Every dream is personal — seek God's Word and the Holy Spirit for confirmation.*

**Date:**       **Time:**       **Dream Title:**

**Dream Description**

**Scriptural Connection**

### Prayer of Revelation
Lord, reveal what You are saying through this dream. Help me to walk in obedience and discern Your will clearly.

**Images/Symbols/Numbers**

**Interpretation/Discernment**

**Emotional Reflection:**

**Action Steps/Application:**
- ◯
- ◯
- ◯
- ◯
- ◯

**Confirmation Notes (Follow Up):**

# AWAKENED WITH PURPOSE

*Every dream is personal — seek God's Word and the Holy Spirit for confirmation.*

**Date:**                    **Time:**                    **Dream Title:**

**Dream Description**

**Scriptural Connection**

### Prayer of Revelation
Lord, reveal what You are saying through this dream. Help me to walk in obedience and discern Your will clearly.

**Images/Symbols/Numbers**

**Interpretation/Discernment**

**Emotional Reflection:**

**Action Steps/Application:**

○
○
○
○
○

**Confirmation Notes (Follow Up):**

# AWAKENED WITH PURPOSE

*Every dream is personal — seek God's Word and the Holy Spirit for confirmation.*

**Date:**                    **Time:**                    **Dream Title:**

**Dream Description**

**Scriptural Connection**

### Prayer of Revelation
Lord, reveal what You are saying through this dream. Help me to walk in obedience and discern Your will clearly.

**Images/Symbols/Numbers**

**Interpretation/Discernment**

**Emotional Reflection:**

**Action Steps/Application:**
- ○
- ○
- ○
- ○
- ○

**Confirmation Notes (Follow Up):**

# AWAKENED WITH PURPOSE

*Every dream is personal — seek God's Word and the Holy Spirit for confirmation.*

**Date:**          **Time:**          **Dream Title:**

**Dream Description**

**Scriptural Connection**

**Prayer of Revelation**
Lord, reveal what You are saying through this dream. Help me to walk in obedience and discern Your will clearly.

**Images/Symbols/Numbers**

**Interpretation/Discernment**

**Emotional Reflection:**

**Action Steps/Application:**
- ○
- ○
- ○
- ○
- ○

**Confirmation Notes (Follow Up):**

May every night become a *sacred conversation.*

May every dream draw you closer to *divine purpose.*

When you rest your head, remember, *God is still talking.*

# Pillow Talk

Pillow Talk was born from those quiet moments when I realized that my dreams were not random, but relational. They were God's gentle conversations — messages of warning, love, and alignment spoken while the noise of the day faded away.

Throughout Scripture, God used dreams to guide His people. Joseph was warned to protect the Messiah, Jacob saw a ladder connecting heaven and earth, Daniel interpreted visions of nations, and Solomon received divine wisdom — all while resting.

The same God who spoke to them still speaks to us today.

This book invites you to slow down, to listen with your spirit, and to recognize that what happens while you sleep may be one of the most important parts of your spiritual life. God desires intimacy — and sometimes, His softest words come when you finally rest your head and surrender.

So tonight, before you close your eyes, whisper this prayer:

*"Speak, Lord. I'm listening — even in my dreams."*

Because when heaven talks, even your pillow becomes holy ground.

www.ingramcontent.com/pod-product-compliance
Lightning Source LLC
Chambersburg PA
CBHW080902120626
46555CB00008B/2910